Present It So They Get It

Create and Deliver Effective PowerPoint Presentations Your Audience Will Understand

Dave Paradi

Other books by Dave Paradi:

The Visual Slide Revolution
102 Tips to Communicate More Effectively Using PowerPoint
Guide to PowerPoint (editions for PowerPoint 2003, 2007 and 2010)
Delivering Your Message With PowerPoint

Published in Canada and the United States
by Communications Skills Press.

Library and Archives Canada Cataloguing in Publication

Paradi, Dave, 1966-
    Present it so they get it : create and deliver effective PowerPoint
presentations your audience will understand / Dave Paradi.

Includes index.
ISBN 978-0-9881549-0-2

    1. Business presentations--Graphic methods--Computer
programs.
2. Microsoft PowerPoint (Computer file). I. Title.

HF5718.22.P375 2012   658.4'52028553   C2012-
906153-0

Printed in Canada and the United States of America

www.PresentItSoTheyGetIt.com

Cover by Rebecca Renner of Creative Minds Inc.

PowerPoint® is a registered trademark of Microsoft Corporation.

Contents

Section Three: Creating Effective Slides

Section Four: How To Start Using These Ideas

Present It So They Get It

Create and Deliver Effective PowerPoint
Presentations Your Audience Will Understand

Acknowledgements

This is my seventh book and I continue to be thankful for my audiences, colleagues in the speaking and presentation professions, and my family.

I continue to be inspired and challenged by those I am fortunate to work with: the organizations who are desperate to improve their presentations; the workshop participants who courageously share their current slides for slide makeovers that demonstrate how they will be able to apply the ideas immediately; and the newsletter subscribers who encourage me even after ten years of writing the bi-weekly newsletter. All of these people push me to deepen my expertise and thinking which benefits future audiences and readers.

My colleagues continue to be shining examples of professionals who inspire me. The presentation professionals who provide wonderful examples of design and approaches that clarify complex ideas. The speakers who take communication and audience connection to new levels. I look forward to gathering with these colleagues every year at conferences and other occasions to share ideas and watch them elegantly demonstrate their craft.

And I continue to be blessed with a family that allows me to do what I do best. My wife, Sheila, provides valuable strategic insight and editing assistance in my work and also keeps our household running while I travel and speak. Our children, Andrew & Laura, understand the challenges of this work and are supportive even when my schedule gets crazy.

Without my family, this book and my work would not be possible. They know how special they are and how thankful I am for their support.

Introduction

The inspiration for this book came from a realization I had sitting in a hotel room in Austin, Texas. I realized that at the core of all presentations is the desire for the audience to understand the message. This may sound obvious, but too much of the effort in presentations today is focused on creating fancier slides or seeing how much information we can pack into the time allotted.

Presenters don't ultimately need fancy slides, cutting edge videos, or new ways to import massive spreadsheets on to a slide. They want the audience to "get it." And the audience wants the same thing. To understand the important message being presented.

So why is it so hard? The media and other commentators continue to claim that the problem is boring presentations. After speaking to thousands of people in workshops and conferences, I have come to the conclusion that this is not the issue. The real problem is that too many presentations are confusing. The audience doesn't "get it" because they are confused by the presentation.

In this book, I set out to give you the practical tools you can use to create a presentation that clearly communicates your message. It will be focused, stripped of excess information, and visually appealing. You do not need to be a designer or graphic artist to create a clear presentation, anyone can use these ideas.

I start by examining what the problem is with presentations today and why presenters create confusing presentations. Then we can start to solve the problems.

It starts with my RAPIDS approach for planning your presentation which will help you create a focused message. Then I show you how to create effective visuals, from slide design that doesn't distract your audience, to creating headlines for your slides, and many examples of visuals with the best practices for creating them. Throughout the chapters, I share examples and case studies so you can see how the ideas work in real life. I end with concrete steps you can take to use the ideas in your own presentations.

I am excited to share this book with you. I hope it gives you the tools and inspiration to create effective presentations that your audience will understand and act on.

Section One:

The Problem With Presentations Today

CHAPTER ONE

Confusing Presentations Are The Problem

According to media commentary and audience members, presentations are not nearly as effective as they could be. People dread going to meetings where the presenter will crank up their laptop and either read from the slides or present volumes of data that don't make sense. Most business people agree that presentations are not often effective in communicating the message. So what is the problem with presentations today?

Many commentators suggest the big problem is that presentations are boring. These commentators recommend solutions to spice up presentations with fancier graphics or tools that make them more entertaining. While I agree that a few presentations might be boring, I don't think that being boring is the primary cause of most ineffective presentations. A boring presentation is one that has no useful information for the audience and is a complete waste of their time. Does this happen? Absolutely. But not very often. My experience is that the presenter does have something valuable to say to this audience. The audience has agreed to hear the presenter because they believe that there will be value in hearing what the presenter has to say. Both presenter and audience want the presentation to succeed, but something goes wrong.

Too many presentations are confusing

The big problem with too many business presentations is that they are confusing, not that they are boring. The audience doesn't leave bored, they leave confused. Their time was wasted not by useless information, but by useful information that was presented so poorly that the time spent gave the audience no value. When executives call me to help their team improve their presentations, it is never because the presentations are boring. It is because the presentations are confusing and not getting the important message across.

One solution to poor presentations according to some commentators is to change the tool you are using. They claim that PowerPoint causes these poor presentations and if you use another tool, it will solve the problem. The problem is not PowerPoint, or any other tool for that matter. PowerPoint does not cause a presenter to fail to properly think through their message. PowerPoint does not cause a presenter to present volumes of data hoping that the audience will figure out the message. PowerPoint does not cause a presenter to ramble through their content with no discernible structure. No, PowerPoint does not cause any of these issues. And no other tool will solve any of these problems. In this book I will refer to PowerPoint as the tool used for business presentations because it is the most common tool. But all the advice applies equally well to any presentation tool you choose to use.

How to tell if your presentation is confusing

How can you tell if your presentation is confusing the audience? One way to tell is to observe the audience during your presentation. Are they engaged and following along? If not, they may be confused. If they have a quizzical look on their faces, or they appear to have mentally checked out, there is a good chance that they are confused. If they are asking basic questions that suggest they did not understand material that you have already presented, it is likely because they are confused. If your presentation is asking for a decision to be made and the decision-maker asks you to gather more input, do more analysis and come back with a new presentation, they may be confused by what you said. It is likely that they think you haven't thought through the request well enough, even though you have done all the relevant analysis already. Have you observed this happening with your audiences? If so, the issue is likely because your presentation is confusing.

Another indication of confusing presentations is observed in situations where you are regularly presenting to the same audience. It could be a monthly update to a management group, quarterly results to a Board of Directors, or bi-weekly executive briefings on a major initiative. You have done a number of these presentations already and they haven't gone as well as you had hoped. The reaction from the senior executives was muted and not as supportive as you would like it to be. Finally, one of the executives approaches you and suggests that in the future, you limit your presentations to no more than five slides. This request to limit the number of slides is usually due to previous presentations that have been confusing. The desire is that limiting the number of slides will force you to become clearer with your message and only present the relevant key points. Unfortunately, most presenters don't understand the request in this way. Their first response is to make the fonts and graphics smaller so they can cram twenty slides of information into the five slide limit. The slides get unreadable, and the reaction from the audience of executives is worse than before. Now they are both confused and unable to read anything on the slides.

Presentations don't have to be confusing

Some presenters know they create confusing presentations and don't know what else to do. They know the reaction from the audience is not what they were hoping for, but they don't know what to change. This can happen when a presenter has seen peers and their boss present in a certain way and figures since others present that way, it must be the most effective way to present the information. They may never have seen a better way. They figure that all presentations are confusing, it is just the nature of presentations. When shown an effective presentation from another industry or situation, they always find an excuse for why that wouldn't work in their presentations. Their presentations are unique and what works elsewhere couldn't possibly work for them. They claim there is nothing they, or anyone else, can do about the confusing presentations. Presenters do not have to accept the status quo of their current presentations. They can make them more effective and less confusing. They can start to set a new standard for presentations in their organization or industry.

CHAPTER TWO

Why Presentations Are Confusing

I don't think presenters set out to create confusing presentations. They truly want to effectively communicate their important message to the audience, but they just don't know how to break some of the habits they have fallen into. In this chapter I want to review some of the most common causes or habits that lead to confusing presentations. In future chapters we will explore how to solve these causes of confusing presentations.

Information overload

In my latest survey of audience members on what annoys them about poor PowerPoint presentations, it was clear that many audience members are fed up with the overload of information presenters are including in presentations. Some commented that presentations have become reports that are read to the audience. I have seen this in my consulting work as well.

Today, more and more presentations have to be e-mailed to those who could not make the live presentation or meeting. As a result, presenters cause information overload by including everything on their slides so that those who only view the slides will be able to understand what was said. Presenters need to make a clear distinction between a report and a presentation. Just because PowerPoint is a presentation software program, this doesn't mean every file created in the software is a presentation. PowerPoint is a tool that can be used to create a presentation or a report. Reports and presentations are two different communication vehicles, each with their own best practices. What works well in a report does not necessarily work well in a presentation. Presenters must be careful to distinguish what vehicle they are using to communicate and not necessarily associate the software used with the type of vehicle being created.

A second cause of information overload is that presenters figure that since they have the information easily accessible in a spreadsheet, they might as well put all of it on slides. Why don't spreadsheets belong on slides? Because a spreadsheet is for calculation, not communication. We use spreadsheets because they are the best tool for analyzing numbers, doing calculations and comparing numeric information. A spreadsheet does those jobs well. It quickly allows us to do hundreds of calculations that would take hours if done by hand. It is so easy to do the calculations that we often end up doing more analysis and obtaining additional insight into the numbers. So for this purpose, a spreadsheet is a great tool.

But when it comes to communicating the results of that analysis to others, the spreadsheet is a terrible tool. It contains far too much detail which confuses instead of informs. The audience only wants the results or conclusions of the analysis, not every step you took to get there. The spreadsheet you used to do the calculations contains both the detailed work and the results, usually with the vast majority of the cells taken up by the details of the analysis, not the resulting conclusions. Presenters need to realize that a spreadsheet is for calculation, not communication.

A third cause of information overload is the belief of some presenters that they need to include every piece of information they have just in case someone might ask about it. Anticipating questions or concerns of the audience is a good and valuable exercise. But discretion needs to be used in determining how much of that analysis is included in the presentation. Often presenters are mistaken that every slide in a PowerPoint file must be shown during the presentation. It is best to have hidden backup slides ready to answer questions if they are asked, instead of overloading the audience with detailed information they may not want to see or hear.

Information overload can also be caused by a misguided belief that the presenter needs to show a lot of information to justify the time spent preparing the measurement and analysis. A presenter may feel that if they don't include all of the work, the audience, usually their boss, won't know how hard they worked. They think that the volume of information in the presentation will help justify their job performance. What they fail to realize is that job performance is measured in many different ways and overloading a presentation does not help ensure a positive performance review.

Contributing to the problem of information overload is an approach we were taught in school of "show your work." When we were in school, the teacher made sure that we showed every step of the assigned question. If we skipped a step, we lost marks. Why did the teacher use this approach? Because their job was to ensure we knew how to do the work. Without seeing every step of our thinking, the teacher could not be sure we understood how to solve the problem or question. When we leave school and enter the world of work, we see our boss as an equivalent to our teacher, and figure they too will want to see every step. Too many presenters fail to realize that in business, we no longer have to show every step of our work. Your boss hired you because they trust that you know how to do the work. They only want to see the result of the work, not every step.

Poor Slide Design

The design of the slides can also contribute to a confusing presentation. While many organizations now have a standard PowerPoint template or master that all staff are to use, presenters still have choices when it comes to choosing colors for diagrams, callouts, graphs and other text and graphics. If the presenter chooses colors that do not have enough contrast, the audience will not be able to clearly distinguish the colors that are beside each other or on top of each other, leading to confusion. In a pie chart for example, if two adjacent pie wedges have similar colors, the audience will not be able to tell the size of each wedge, which is the most important part of interpreting a pie chart. When the text color does not have enough contrast with the background color the audience can't read the text and misses the meaning. This can occur in a text box, a shape, or a diagram. In Chapter 10, I will introduce you to a tool that ensures the colors you select will be easy for the audience to see.

Another aspect of slide design that can cause confusion for the audience is the selection of font for text on the slides. By selecting fonts that are easy to read, display properly on all computers, and are large enough to be easily seen, your text will not confuse the audience. In Chapter 10, I will discuss font selection in more detail.

Confusing Visuals

I advocate for more use of visuals instead of slides full of text. But some presenters use visuals in a way that confuses the audience. The most common cause of a confusing visual is overloading the slide so the point of the slide becomes impossible to comprehend. It can be an overload of text, graphics, or both that cause the audience to be confused. When a slide has too much on it, the audience takes one look, decides that it is too hard to even attempt to understand, and mentally checks out.

The second type of confusing visual is one that the audience doesn't understand because it is the wrong choice of visual for the message being conveyed. For example, if you are trying to show the market share of four products in a single region, a line chart would not be the correct choice because it does not allow the audience to see the comparison between the four products. A pie chart would be the correct choice of visual in this situation. Selecting the visuals used without careful consideration of whether the visual will communicate the key message results in audience confusion. In Chapter 12 I will give advice on how to select the appropriate visual for the message you are trying to communicate.

Lack of preparation

Successful presenters don't just show up and deliver the presentation. The success of their presentation is based on exacting preparation that leads to a confidence in what they are saying and how it will be presented. Too often, the first time a presenter delivers their presentation is when they are in front of the audience. This is known as "practicing live" and can lead to audience confusion. Since the presenter has not practiced what they will say, they are flying by the seat of their pants and things don't always go well. Presenters realize what would have made the presentation better and comment after the presentation, "I wish I had thought of saying that during the presentation." The only way to be truly ready to present is to rehearse the presentation by delivering it out loud well ahead of the presentation date. Test how words and phrases sound, whether there is a better way to say what you want, and get the timing down so you don't run over the time allocated for your presentation. After you have rehearsed the presentation a few times, you can then determine if you are ready or could benefit with further rehearsals. Work until you feel comfortable that it is a conversation with the audience.

If a presenter has not prepared well, they aren't ready to expand on the information on the slides and they end up simply reading the slides to the audience. In my latest survey of over 600 audience members, almost three quarters said that the speaker reading the slides is by far the top annoyance with poor PowerPoint presentations. If you are just reading the slides, you aren't doing a presentation. You are reading a report, which is a waste of everyone's time. It can confuse the audience because they are not sure why they are there if they could have read your report as an email attachment. When you are asked to deliver a presentation, build time in to your schedule to start working on the message and accompanying visuals well before the presentation date. By booking time in your schedule, you set aside the requisite preparation time to ensure that you have structured a clear message and are so familiar with your material that you won't need to rely on reading the slides.

The final aspect of preparation that can lead to audience confusion is the presenter not taking control of the room from well before the presentation begins. When a presenter arrives three minutes before their presentation is to start, fumbles with setting up the equipment, and isn't ready to begin, the audience is thrown off and distracted by the environment surrounding the presentation. You should aim to arrive at least 30 to 60 minutes ahead of your scheduled presentation time in order to make sure the setup is done properly. Test everything from microphones to projectors to the room setup. Adjust any aspects of the room that need to be changed in order for the audience to get the most from your time with them. Make sure that your speaking space is set up for success: speaking notes easily seen and pages easily moved as you proceed through the presentation, glass of water nearby to keep your throat lubricated, any cords or wires taped down so you don't trip, and knowledge of where you can move without blocking some audience members. By removing all the possible distractions that can cause an audience to not fully pay attention to your presentation, you can reduce the probability that the audience leaves confused.

With all of the reasons that confusing presentations are so common, you may initially be discouraged. Don't be. While the reasons may be many, I believe that the issues can be solved, and, with practice, you can form the habits that will lead to future successful presentations. In Section Two I will share details of the RAPIDS approach that will help you plan your message and the delivery of your presentation. In Section Three, I will show you how to create effective slides to visually support the message.

Section Two:

The RAPIDS Approach
To Planning A Presentation

Introduction To The RAPIDS Approach

The most important aspect of any presentation is being clear about your message. I have found that too many presenters start preparing their presentation by first creating PowerPoint slides. Once they have slides created or copied from a previous presentation, they try to fit the slides in to a coherent message. This takes a lot of time and results in a less effective presentation. Instead, presenters should work on the message first, then create slides to support that message.

To help presenters start in the correct place, I have created a structured approach, summarized using the acronym RAPIDS, that will help you focus your message and determine what slides you need for your presentation. By investing some time up front on your message, you will cut down the overall time you spend creating presentations. I will introduce the steps in the RAPIDS approach here and then each step will be more fully discussed in Chapters 3 to 9.

R – Real Goal

The goal of your presentation is the foundation of everything else that you do in the presentation, so you need a solid goal that will support the rest of the content. Too often presenters are not clear about the goal of the presentation and it leads to a lot of wasted effort. Ultimately it contributes to a disappointing outcome when the audience does not understand the message.

A – Audience analysis

The audience should be at the center of everything we do as presenters. Too often a presentation is created without regard to the specific audience who will be seeing the presentation, or the presentation is created with the desire that it should fit every possible audience who might see it. As a presenter we need to analyze the audience for each presentation and make decisions about how to best serve that audience.

P – Presentation outline

The content of the presentation needs to be structured in a way that will be easy for the audience to follow. A good outline organizes the main points and supporting information so it is logical and flows smoothly from the beginning to the end of the presentation.

I – Information that is laser focused

This is where presenters need to solve the information overload problem that causes so much of the confusion in presentations today. There are a number of strategies that you can use to decide what information should be part of your presentation and what should be left out. You will find that by focusing your content, the message is clearly understood.

D – Detailed plan for each slide

A lot of the time spent creating slides is wasted because the presenter doesn't have a good idea of what they want the slide to look like. Once you have a detailed outline of the topics you want to present, you should create a detailed plan for each slide: how it will look, what it will say, and how you will present it. Creating effective slides does not require graphics or design training.

S – Sufficiently prepared to present

Presenters deliver confidently because they have planned their preparation from the start and know on the day of the presentation that they have done everything they can to make this presentation a success. This includes planning time for rehearsals, using checklists for their content and technology, and making sure they are set up well before the presentation is to begin.

By using the RAPIDS approach to planning your presentation, you address the issues of information overload and lack of preparation that can lead to confusing presentations.

Case Studies Using The RAPIDS Approach

The RAPIDS approach has been proven to work in the consulting assignments I complete for my clients. Here are three examples of these steps applied to create successful presentations.

Case Study #1: Market Research Firm

Problem: This firm was invited to present their qualifications to a very large potential client. The majority of the time spent in front of the prospect was to be the presentation itself, so it needed to get the executives interested in what the firm could provide. The first draft of their presentation was primarily a copy of the text and graphics off their website. It was far too wordy and not convincing at all.

Solution: Using the RAPIDS approach, I helped them think through what was unique about their services and how it would solve a large problem for this prospective client. We revamped the entire structure of the message and created more effective graphics that eliminated a lot of the text. They felt that it flowed much better and really highlighted their unique services.

Outcome: The presentation went very well with the executives engaged and asking good questions after the presentation. Within three weeks of the presentation, the market research firm received an invitation to quote on a significant piece of business and the principal of the firm said in an e-mail "the presentation you helped us with worked."

Case Study #2: Insurance Agency

Problem: The owner of a small boutique insurance agency was asked to present a bid for mandatory insurance that an organization was required to purchase. The other firm invited to bid was a much larger agency with more resources available to apply to the presentation. The owner asked me to help him develop a presentation that would win the business.

Solution: After discussions with the owner, we determined that the goal of the presentation was to convince the Board of Directors, who would be making the decision after seeing both presentations, of the best criteria to use when making the decision. If they used the right criteria, the owner knew that his proposal would come out on top. We designed a presentation that not only presented why certain criteria were best for the organization to use, but how the agency's proposal exceeded those criteria with proven examples.

Outcome: The presentation went very well and the next day, the owner got a call from the Board saying that his proposal had been selected. The owner attributes significant credit to the planning and approach of the presentation.

Case Study #3: Conference Presentation

Problem: The head of an organization was making a presentation at a conference of marketing executives who could be potential clients. If her message on the current situation and opportunities was clear and made an impact, future prospects would arise. Her initial draft presentation was filled with data tables and text that would overwhelm the audience.

Solution: Although the overall structure was set, we worked within each section to focus the information into what this audience would really need to hear. We eliminated a lot of numbers and created graphs or visuals instead of some of the tables of data.

Outcome: In an e-mail sent to me later the same day after her presentation, she said, "My presentation this a.m. went very well! It was a 1,000 times better than it would have been without your help." By reducing the information down to just what the audience needed to know, it made her job as a presenter easier. She could focus on making the message come alive without being burdened by the data.

These case studies illustrate that focusing your message and using effective slides make your presentation more successful. It is easier for you to present and your audience will walk away with a clear understanding of your message. The following chapters detail each step of the RAPIDS approach.

CHAPTER THREE

R – Real Goal

The foundation of your presentation should be a clear, realistic statement of the goal of this presentation. I see the goal of a presentation as the destination of a journey you want to take the audience on. If you are using a GPS device, the first thing it asks you for is your destination. And it has to be a specific destination in order for the directions to be accurate. Just specifying a town or a street is not enough. It looks for a specific address. Think of this when considering the goal of your presentation.

Too often I hear presenters say that they are presenting an update, or they are presenting on a topic because they were asked to. If you can only answer "what" you are presenting on, you haven't gone far enough. I suggest that the real goal of your presentation also includes "why" you are presenting, in addition to "what" you are presenting. You aren't just presenting a project update, you are doing the presentation to gain continued support for the current project or perhaps get a critical decision made so that you can move forward. You aren't just presenting the quarterly financial or operating results, you are presenting the insights that give executives the confidence to make decisions that will positively impact the future results.

One way to get clear on the goal of your presentation is to finish this sentence: At the end of the presentation, the audience will _____. What will the audience do, know, understand, agree to, approve, etc.? What action do you want the audience to take at the end of your presentation? It seems like answering this question would be easy, but in many cases it is harder than you think. In speaking with cancer researchers who present their research findings at conferences, they suggested that at the end of the presentation their audience would know about their research. I told them that this was not enough. It did not include the "why" of the presentation. They needed to look at what they wanted the audience to do, which may be to continue to fund the research, support them with other types of resources, or partner on future research projects. Take some time to consider the real goal of your presentation.

Another way to look at the importance of the goal of your presentation is to return to the concept of the goal being the foundation of your presentation. The foundation of a building needs to be solid enough to support what is built on top of it. Would you rather build a house on a foundation of concrete or a foundation of sand? The concrete foundation will be stable and support the home. The goal of your presentation needs to support the content you will create and deliver.

Make sure you are clear and not abstract when stating the goal. Use measurable language, not flowery language that sounds good but means little. For example, saying that the goal of your presentation is to have the team excited about the new product launch is not specific enough. It sounds good, but won't result in any action. What do you want them to do with the excitement? Instead, decide the goal is the team will be motivated to book a meeting with ten customers within two to four weeks following the presentation to discuss the new product. That is specific, not flowery, and can be measured.

Coming up with the goal for your presentation is not necessarily simple, but it is important and an excellent investment of your time. If you have been asked to create a presentation for someone else, ask them what the goal is so that the time you spend working on the presentation is productive. Ask additional questions until they can clearly state the goal in specific language as we have talked about. This will help you know how to spend your time preparing the presentation.

When a presenter skips this step of determining the real goal of their presentation, it is obvious because the presentation rambles through topics with no clear destination. This type of presentation is confusing and does not benefit the audience. Remember to invest time up front for this important first step in planning your presentation.

CHAPTER FOUR

A – Audience Analysis

Whether it is a few people around a boardroom table or hundreds of people in a conference ballroom, your audience should always be the primary focus of your presentation. Part of keeping the audience as the primary focus is to make sure everything you do in the presentation is there to benefit the audience, not there because you, the presenter, think it is "cool." One of the tools I use to help me is a question that acts as a filter. A filter works by removing those elements that are harmful and only allowing the beneficial elements to pass through the filter. This question can help you decide whether a point, a slide element or presentation technique should be included in your presentation. Here's the question to use as a filter: "How will this help the audience understand the message better?"

This question should always be in your mind when considering any aspect of your presentation. Your content, each element of your slides and everything you do in delivering the slides should be focused on helping the audience understand the key points you are trying to make. In order to make effective use of this filter, you need to know more about your audience, so you can make decisions that benefit them.

You should never give a "canned" presentation, one that is the same, no matter to what audience you deliver it. Why? Because each audience is different. As the presenter, you need to know where this audience is now if you are going to move them to the goal that you set for the presentation. Earlier, we talked about setting the destination for a presentation in terms of what you want the audience to do at the end of it. As with any trip or journey, if you don't know where you are starting from, you won't know what route to take in order to reach your destination.

How can you determine where the audience is now? There are a number of dimensions to consider. First, find out who will be at the presentation. What is their position in the organization, what role do they play, what level of decision-making power or influence do they have, and where geographically do they come from? All of these factors can inform you as to what you may need to include in your presentation and whom you may need to pay more attention to in the room, since these key audience members are more critical to the success of your presentation.

Second, determine what their level of knowledge is on the topic. When thinking about knowledge level, consider both real knowledge and the level of knowledge they think they have – these two levels are frequently not the same. It is quite common that someone thinks they know more than they do. If you believe this to be true, don't embarrass them by pointing this out. Incorporate phrases such as, "As you probably already know …", to convey information without them losing face in front of their peers. If the audience as a whole has a lower level of knowledge on this topic than your usual audiences, this suggests that you may need to cover some of the "basics" at the start of the presentation, so that everyone gets up to speed, before proceeding with more complex information. You also need to consider their literacy level. Your audience may consist of people who don't understand the language very well because they come from different countries. Or your audience may have a low level of reading comprehension and require explanations that are not text based.

Third, get a sense of their attitude towards your topic and your position on that topic. You may discover that some audience members do not like your topic area or are opposed to your viewpoint. Before a session in Jacksonville, I had a man approach me and say, "Just so you know, Dave, I hate PowerPoint!" I quickly became clear what his attitude was towards my topic! This allowed me at the start of the session to address some of the concerns that he and other audience members had, which diffused some of the tension and allowed us to move on. You may need to do the same in your presentation. By thinking through the objections and concerns of the audience, you can determine what content you should include that will answer those questions before they are raised.

Fourth, evaluate your level of credibility and trust with this group. If it is a group of colleagues you work with regularly, you may not need to address this issue at all because they know you. But if it is a group who has never heard of you or your organization, you will have to build credibility from the start. Build trust through your introduction and add some information throughout proving that you are an expert on this topic and worth listening to.

Finally, consider what style or format this group prefers for presentations. Some groups, such as a Board of Directors, usually expect pre-reading before they see a presentation. Whenever you provide pre-reading, analyze whether this audience will actually have read the material before you present. If they have likely read your material in advance, start your presentation assuming that they are ready to hear the next steps.

Some industries expect presentations done in a particular format. One of the industries I work with uses PowerPoint a lot, but they never project their presentations. They only print the slides one per page and bind the pages along the long edge into a "flipbook." The presentations are done across a boardroom table with each person flipping through their copy of the book. For these types of presentations, you will need to design the presentation accordingly. The other aspect of presentation style to consider is whether the audience expects a handout or not. If the audience expects a handout, spend time determining what type of handout they will find most helpful. It may be a copy of your slides, or it may be a document that they can use as a reference document to implement what you have presented. It is important to present in the format or style that the audience is comfortable with to show that you are familiar with them and their issues.

By considering who will be in the audience, what their level of knowledge is, what their concerns or objections are to what you are presenting, your level of credibility with this audience, and what this audience expects in terms of presentation style or format, you will be better prepared to decide what content you need to include in your presentation.

CHAPTER FIVE

P – Presentation Outline

Creating an outline for your presentation is a process of determining all of the content for the presentation. It starts at a high level and proceeds to greater levels of detail, resulting in a well organized detailed outline. The outline process also includes the important aspects of how you will be introduced, how you will grab attention at the start of the presentation, and how you will end the presentation.

Map your presentation

The GPS analogy that I introduced earlier is also valuable in outlining how to move the audience from where they are now to where you want them to be at the end of your presentation. Once a GPS knows the destination and starting point, it can lay out a map of how you will make the journey. You should do the same for your presentation and map out the journey you want to take the audience on.

A map has different levels of detail, and so should your presentation outline. The highest level of your presentation outline consists of the few major areas or topics you will cover. This is similar to the list of towns that a map contains. The next level of detail contains the specific points you intend to share within each topic. This would be the roads on a map. The most detailed level of your presentation outline is the supporting information or facts that further explain the points you are making. On a map, these details are similar to specific road information such as whether it is a one-way street or a gravel road.

Just as a map logically organizes a geographic region, your presentation outline should logically flow from point to point within a topic and from one topic to the next. This map of your presentation helps you keep on track and makes sure you are moving the audience towards the intended destination.

I suggest sharing the map with your audience at the start of your presentation in the form of the agenda or list of key topics you will cover. This gives the audience an idea of how things will flow and they know what journey they are on. They can then consider each of the topics as a signpost along the route. Every time you move to the next topic in your presentation, use a title slide to indicate that you are moving to the next topic. These title slides are the signposts the audience will be looking for and it guides them along the way.

Sequencing your points

Research by Michael Posner, cited by John Medina in his book *Brain Rules*, says that our brains retain the overall meaning of an experience at the expense of remembering all the details. This means that the audience will remember the conclusion but not necessarily all the data that backs it up. That may be good for us as presenters because we want the audience to remember our key message.

The problem comes when that conclusion is buried deep in our presentation. Too often the typical sequence of a presentation is to present every supporting data point before we present the conclusion. By the time we get to the most important part, our audience is overwhelmed and may miss the conclusion or not recognize the significance of it.

I suggest that to improve the effectiveness of your presentations, start by stating the conclusion. Give the audience a clear idea of what the destination of this presentation is. Then you can support this conclusion with data presented in an order that logically supports the conclusion. Once they know where you are going, it is much easier for the audience to understand how the data you are presenting substantiates the conclusion you have already stated. And they remember that key message better because it was presented first and backed up second.

You may be concerned that if you present the conclusion first, the audience may not want to pay attention to the rest of the presentation or they may immediately start asking questions if they don't agree with the conclusion. I suggest that you can keep their attention by stating that the rest of the presentation will provide detailed support for the conclusion and that you would be happy to take questions after they have heard the details so that they have the proper context for a deeper discussion. Most people will want to hear the rest of your message so that they can come to their own conclusion and then discuss it with you.

One option that you may want to consider is a non-linear presentation. In this type of presentation, you start with the overall conclusion and main supporting points, but then ask the audience what additional details they would like to hear from a menu of topics you give them. The audience selects the topic that is most important to them at this time. When you have finished presenting that topic, you return to the menu of choices and allow the audience to select the next topic. The audience continues directing you until they are satisfied or have covered all of the choices on the menu.

This type of presentation totally engages the audience because they are in control of what is covered and the order. They may change their mind on what information they need to hear based on what you said in a previous section. They will end the presentation when they want to, satisfied that they have been given the information they need to act on your message. When the presentation ends may have nothing to do with how much time was allotted to the presentation at the start.

I have seen this type of presentation work well in a sales scenario. The presenter talked about how his firm could solve each of the top four challenges in the industry, and then asked which of the four challenges was the most critical for the client at this time. He could then go into more detail on the solutions offered in that area. It was very effective and led to a deeper conversation with the client than a standard presentation would have provided.

A non-linear presentation is built using the hyperlink feature of PowerPoint, which allows you to jump to any slide in the presentation. You design modules in the file and add hyperlinks that allow you to move between the menu and each module, then back to the menu. It does not require fancy programming, but it requires a little more planning. Depending on the order that the audience chooses, you may need to recap some material at the start of each module. This helps the audience have the necessary background information for each module no matter what order the modules are presented in.

The first time you deliver a non-linear presentation, it can be a little scary. You are giving up control to the audience and have to be prepared to go wherever they want to go. But you will find that a non-linear presentation can be more effective in certain situations because the audience is engaged and walks out knowing that they got what they came for.

Supporting information

For each of the points you will cover, you will use supporting information to explain the point in more detail. This can include expert opinions, articles or news stories, facts and statistics you have calculated, government or research information, or case studies and examples. When evaluating data that you or others have calculated, always check the calculations. Perform spot checks of data that has been transcribed to make sure there are no errors. Check the formulas to make sure that the right components have been included and calculated properly. Do a reasonability test against other known data to see if these calculations fit a larger pattern. These checks and others that may be specific to your type of data are even more crucial when you are presenting something that is contrary to what has been accepted in the past.

When you find a fact, statistic, or example, especially if you find it on the Internet, how do you verify that it is true? Why should you even bother to verify it? Because if you don't, your presentation may not be successful. If you present a "fact" that the audience knows is not true based on their background or knowledge, they may doubt what you say and place little confidence in the rest of your presentation.

When searching for information on the Internet, there are a few ways to assure yourself that what you are finding is actually true. First, look for the source of the data. If you read an article or fact that is not sourced, treat it with suspicion. A good author will always cite the source of the data so that it can be checked. When you see a source cited, see if you can go back to that source document to make sure that the author has used the data in the way that the researcher had intended and the data has not been taken out of context.

Second, when you find data or information online, make sure you evaluate the site it is coming from. I suggest you place higher value on sites that adhere to publishing standards. Sites such as those from educational institutions (.edu at the end of the URL is one indicator of educational institution websites), government sites, refereed academic journals and major newspapers or magazines all have standards that require articles to be independently verified before being published. While this is not an absolute guarantee of truthfulness, it at least assures you that some verification has been done and your risk of the information being fictitious is reduced.

Create a detailed outline

Now that you have considered the best sequence for the points and gathered the information you want to include in your presentation, the next step is to create a detailed outline of your presentation. Organize the topics, points, and supporting information using one of the following effective methods:

1) Use an outlining format in mind mapping software. This allows you to associate each point and supporting information with the topic it is associated with.

2) Use sticky notes or notecards to lay out the entire presentation under your main topics. You can arrange the topics across the top of the desk or wall, and then place each point and associated supporting information underneath the appropriate topic in an order that makes sense.

3) Use a table layout in a word processor. Set up a table on a wide landscape page so that you can have five columns on the page in a readable font size. Each column represents one of the topics and the points and supporting information are arranged underneath these main area headings.

Here is an example of a presentation outline using sticky notes or notecards (different shapes have been used to make the levels in the outline easier to distinguish):

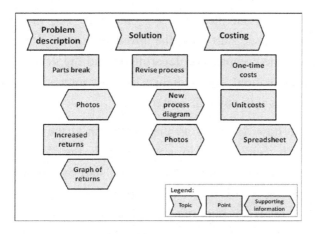

These breakdown methods give you a great visual way to see your entire presentation and make changes to the sequence, or add to areas that need more points or supporting information. This overall view also allows you to review the presentation outline with others to get their input and opinion. It is easier at this point to make changes to the structure, instead of investing time creating slides and then realizing that major changes are required.

Now that you have created a detailed outline of your content, take some time to consider three critical parts of your presentation, your opening, your closing, and how you will be introduced before you speak.

Grab attention with your opening

Presenters often ask, "What is the best way to start my presentation?" The different methods they tried haven't worked out as well as they had hoped. It is critical that you grab the audience's attention with your opening so they know why they are there and what they will get out of it. Too many of the presentations I see start with: the introduction of the team, many facts about the company or department, and the detailed agenda of the presentation. The audience has lost interest by the time you actually get to any real content.

So how do you grab their attention at the start of your presentation, and what do you do with the "company" or "organization" information? You should start by making it clear to the audience why they should spend time listening to you. What key analysis, important decision, or future direction are you going to discuss that will directly impact this audience? Base your opening on the presentation goal you set earlier. Unless they see the connection to their own lives, they won't see a reason to stay tuned to the rest of the presentation. This is why I previously suggested starting with the conclusion, it brings the item of greatest interest front and center.

Once you have started with the reason they should pay attention, you can then share the agenda to give the audience a roadmap to follow during the presentation. Don't go into detail with the agenda, keep it to the main areas you will cover. I saw a one hour presentation that had a seven slide agenda; the audience is looking for the exit by slide four because they are overwhelmed already.

Consider whether you really need to include the "organization" information, all those details about the team or company. Many times that information is self-serving and does not really help the audience understand your message (remember the filter I talked about earlier). If you do include this type of information, it must be presented in a way that your audience understands why it matters to them, not just because you are trying to boast.

The old methods you may have heard of, such as telling a joke, commenting on the news, or reciting how great we are do not work. Our audience expects to be engaged from the start. If we don't engage them, they will turn to their laptop, smartphone, or even get up and leave. Start your presentation with why your topic is important to this audience and you will have a more successful presentation.

Close strongly with a "call to action"

In my opinion, the worst way to end your presentation is with a slide that screams, "Questions???" or, "Thanks!!!" When you finish with a slide that says "Questions???", it suggests to the audience that you know you weren't clear and you know they should have questions on what you presented. With the last slide saying "Thanks!!!", it says to the audience that you are thankful that the audience showed up and did not leave. With either of these endings, you leave the audience in a state of doubt about what you want them to do next. Neither of these endings successfully reaches the goal that you set for the presentation because it leaves the audience hanging and possibly confused.

What is a more effective way to conclude your presentation? Assume that the audience understood what you said and be ready to discuss what comes next. Have a "call to action" that moves them to the goal you set for the presentation.

If you are doing a training or informational presentation, ask the audience how they will use the information you have shared. In a status update presentation, ask for a sign of support to proceed with the direction you have suggested. If you are asking for approval of a recommendation, be specific in asking for the decision to be made.

The way you conclude your presentation is critically important to how the audience perceives the entire presentation. Don't end with a weak closing that leaves the audience confused and unlikely to act on your message. Finish strongly with confidence in what you said and ensuring the audience takes action on your ideas.

Effective introductions before you speak

Far too often, the effectiveness of your presentation is undermined by a poor introduction. Why do poor introductions hurt your message? Because they take too long, they share information that is not important to the presentation and they have the wrong focus. I suggest that whenever you are being introduced before a presentation, that you write your own introduction and ask it to be read as written. Here's what I think should be in that introduction.

The first priority of your introduction is to share with the audience why they should listen to you. The introduction needs to overcome the skepticism they may have as to why they should spend their valuable time listening to you. You need to build credibility in the introduction. The audience wants to know what significant results you have produced, what degrees, designations or certificates you have that are relevant to the topic, and what similar work you have done in the past that shows familiarity with these issues.

Next, your introduction should set the stage for your presentation. Explain why your topic is important at this time and how your presentation will benefit the audience. This does not need to be more than one or two sentences.

Finally, the introduction should invite the speaker to start. The entire introduction should be sixty seconds or less. The audience wants to hear what you have to say, not listen to an introduction drone on and on. Remember that an effective introduction is not about you, it is about the benefits and value you will deliver to this audience.

When you are presenting with others in a multi-presenter session, how do you hand the presentation off to the next presenter? Unfortunately, the most common introduction sounds something like, "Oh, this is your slide Leslie; I guess it's your turn now." Does that set up the next presenter for success? No. And it reduces the effectiveness of the overall presentation.

In a multi-presenter situation, the introductions need to be even briefer than a single presenter because it will otherwise interrupt the flow of the overall presentation. The aim should be for 15 to 30 seconds or less. Here is an example:

"As compelling as the operational advantages of this initiative are, we know that you are also concerned about the financial impact of the work. I'd like to ask Eric to come and talk about the financial analysis he has done that shows how this project is a high return initiative. Eric has an MBA and has provided solid analysis that we have based our own decisions on for two years. Eric, walk us through this next section please."

There are a number of things to notice in this example:

1. There is a tie to the previous section. To give the audience context for why the next presenter should be speaking, the previous presenter needs to set up why the next topic is relevant and important at this time in the presentation.

2. It positions why the audience should listen by previewing the key point that the next presenter will be speaking to. This gets the audience primed to listen to the support for the conclusion that they have been given.

3. It positions the next presenter as the expert in the topic by explaining that they are the ones who have done the analysis and their advice has been relied on in the past. It also gives any relevant education or external qualifications. If external qualifications are not available, reference internal ones.

4. It invites the next presenter to start right away with the topic at hand. The audience does not want to have

breaks in the flow, so they want the presenter to get right to the points they are going to share.

These introductions should be practiced and rehearsed in advance. Don't think that you can just "wing it" on the day of the presentation. You will forget a part or forget to introduce the person at all. Also, don't just stumble through a printed introduction. If you need to read it because you won't be able to remember it, include it in your normal speaking notes and refer to it just like you would refer to your notes for any slide you are delivering. It should seem natural and flow like all the rest of your points. You are the one who will convince the audience that the next presenter is an expert.

A key component to making multi-presenter presentations effective is to develop and deliver the introductions so they create a smooth transition for the audience from section to section. Prepare for this part of your presentation just as you prepare for the content you will be delivering. It will make your presentation more effective and show how well your team works together.

Creating a detailed presentation outline that contains all of the content you plan to cover is a crucial step in making sure that your presentation reaches its goal. The outline should include the topics, points, and supporting information you want to include in the presentation, along with how you will open and close the presentation.

CHAPTER SIX

I – Information That Is Laser Focused

Presenters often identify and include too much information in the detailed outline of their presentation. Information overload is the biggest issue in presentations today according to the audiences that I speak to and survey. People are leaving presentations confused because they can't make sense of the volume of information being presented. The unfortunate thing is that many presenters don't know that they are overloading their audience with information. In Chapter 2, I reviewed how to tell if you are confusing your audience with too much information.

You may not think that the audience being confused by an overload of information is that big of a deal. Here is why you should care: A confused mind never makes a decision. Read that statement again. In many cases we are asking our audiences to make a decision. To use a new work procedure, to approve a project, to buy our products or services, to continue to support our initiative, to support our cause, or any number of other decisions that we ask our audiences to make. If they are confused, they won't make the decision. They will delay, ask for more information, or even go in a different direction, one they feel is safer, with less risk to them because they are comfortable with it, even though it may not be as good of a decision. If we want to reach the goal of our presentation, we need to solve the information overload problem. Let's look at five strategies for doing just this.

Strategy 1: The Questioning Strategy

This strategy involves honest answers to some very direct questions. The purpose of the questions is to get you to make difficult decisions on what content really needs to be part of your presentation. I know that making a decision to leave content out of your presentation is difficult. It is an emotional decision because you have spent time and effort in creating the content and feel emotionally invested in it. Adopting a truly audience centered viewpoint can help make these decisions a little easier.

Question 1: Does this move the audience closer to the goal of the presentation?

The goal of the presentation is to move the audience from where they are now to where we want them to be, using the map that we talked about earlier. Just like any journey, if you don't keep moving towards the destination, you wander off course and get lost. This is what happens to the audience when we include information that is not totally focused on moving the message forward. If it takes the audience down a different route, while that might be a scenic route, it serves to confuse the audience. If we decide that we should say something a second time in a different way just in case they didn't get it the first time, we confuse the audience. Ultimately we need to ask ourselves, "If I left it out, would they still understand?" If the answer is "yes", then leave it out and move on.

Question 2: Is this a summary/result of the work, or the details of how the work was done?

It is common to have done a lot of analysis and many calculations in preparing for your presentation. Too often presenters think that they should present all this detail and let the audience figure the point out, since the conclusion should be obvious. It is unlikely that the audience will do the work to determine the point. They expect you, as the presenter, to have summarized the analysis into a clearly explained conclusion. Presenters also think that it is important for the audience to hear about all the assumptions, steps in the process, formulas, and calculations. You may also be tempted to include who did each step, how long it took, when it was done and even what office location helped out. While all of this information may be important to you, the truth is that the audience doesn't need to hear it all.

What your audience needs to hear is the conclusion you reached. What does your work mean to them with respect to the problem they are trying to solve? How will your work help them make an important decision they are facing? They want to know the bottom line, not all the lines in between. The focus of your presentation should be on the conclusion of your work, not the details of your work. They trust that you did the work properly, that's why they asked you to do this analysis.

But what about all the details? Shouldn't we include some details? Only include those few details that, if changed, would significantly impact the conclusion. Talk about a key assumption you used that, if not correct, would change the whole outcome. Review the source of an input that some may want to question. When you review these areas of possible contention, also discuss how you verified the decisions you made so that further questions don't need to arise. Other than those key details that impact the conclusion, leave out the rest of the details.

But what about all the work the team did in coming up with the conclusion? If we only present the final conclusion, the audience won't know all the work we put in. If we have many slides showing everything we did, then the audience will know how much work we did. If you are including detail just to show how much work was done, please don't. The audience will be able to tell the depth of the work by how well the conclusion helps them and how well you explain the impact of your conclusion. Executives and managers evaluate the quantity and quality of work by many methods that rarely include how many slides of detail are in your presentation.

Question 3: Am I including this information just in case they ask?

Presenters are often concerned that they should include every detail just in case someone asks about one of the steps or a formula they used. You should anticipate possible questions and prepare answers for them. Those answers should not be part of your core presentation. If you want to include a slide that will help answer the question, create a hidden slide that you can quickly jump to if the question gets asked. A hidden slide is one that is part of your presentation file, but does not get displayed in Slide Show mode unless you specifically access it. You access these hidden slides in two common ways. First, you can include a hyperlink on the slide you think may trigger that question. During the presentation, if the question does not get raised, you just proceed with the next topic. If someone does ask the question, you can activate the hyperlink, which takes you to the hidden slide that helps answer the question. I suggest you place the hidden slide right after the slide that may raise that question. This way, once you are done answering the question, you can simply proceed to the next slide to continue your presentation. If you put all the hidden slides at the end of the file, you have to add a hyperlink back to where you want to continue the presentation, which is more work.

The second method for jumping to a hidden slide is to use the ability of PowerPoint to jump to any slide from any point in the presentation. The two options for jumping to any slide in PowerPoint are described in the Delivery Skills section of Chapter 8.

If you anticipate that the answer may need even deeper explanation or a more interactive discussion than is possible on a hidden slide, you can also use a hyperlink to open another document or spreadsheet. If you need to capture ideas or review a document to answer a question or objection, you can set up a hyperlink on your slide to open an existing word processor document or PDF document. If someone is questioning how a change in an assumption would change your conclusion, you can jump right to the spreadsheet and do the calculation live, right in front of the audience. When you hyperlink to an outside file from a PowerPoint slide, it opens the file in the appropriate program on top of your presentation that is running. You have full access to all features of the program to make changes or view other areas of the document or spreadsheet. Once you are done, you can save any changes, and exit the application. Once the application closes, you are returned to your presentation, and can continue with the next slide. I will discuss hyperlinks in more detail in Chapter 18.

These techniques allow you to have the comfort of the detailed information at hand, without overwhelming the audience with information that will confuse them and cause them not to understand your message.

Strategy 2: The Three R's of focusing your point

In data dump presentations, we see slides that have too many words and too many bullet points. This confuses the audience because they don't know what is the most important information. When I ask presenters to reduce the number of points and words, a common complaint is that they don't know how to reduce the twelve bullet points they have on their overloaded slide down to the three that the audience really needs to know about. To help you focus all your points, let me suggest a three step process that can help you realize what information the audience really needs to know. Each of these steps starts with the letter R, so I refer to these as the three R's of focusing your points.

Rank

The first step is to rank your points based on the importance to your audience. Don't try to tell me that all the points are of equal importance, because they aren't. If you are having trouble ranking the points, go back and look at the topic from the perspective of the audience. What are the critical points they need to know about this topic? Rank your points from most important to least important. If you want to combine some points because they relate to a larger issue, feel free to do so. When you are done, you will have a list of points ranked by importance.

Reduce

Now that the points are ranked, reduce them to the top two or three points. This is even harder than ranking because you will have to eliminate some or many of the points you originally wanted to include. Consider how you would answer this question: "If you could only tell the audience one point, what would it be?" This examination again may lead you to combining one point with another to create a more important topic. You may not be restricted to only one point, but this exercise forces you to make the hard choices that the audience expects every presenter to make.

Rephrase

Now that you have only two or three key points, restate them in terms of why the point matters to the audience. Make sure you haven't just stated a fact or data, but, instead, what that fact or data means to your audience. Make sure that each point relates in some way to moving the audience towards the goal you set for this presentation.

Once you have gone through the three R's process, you will have a more focused slide containing the key information the audience needs to know. Your audience will clearly understand your message and you can focus your preparation on only those points that matter the most.

Strategy 3: Moving from Data to Information to Insight

As I said previously, spreadsheets are for calculations, not communications. The audience doesn't want to see the entire spreadsheet on a slide. They expect you to figure out the conclusion from the analysis. That requires more than just a spreadsheet. When you are presenting numeric information in a presentation, it is important that you move through the three stages of analysis to ensure that the audience understands your message. The three stages of analysis are:

Data

Data are the raw numbers that you have measured. This can be collected from a financial system, an operational control system, personal observations and measurements or a variety of other methods. On their own, data does not have meaning. A number by itself cannot have meaning unless you move to the next stage of analysis.

Information

Data is turned into information by comparing it to some desired state. The desired state could be a goal, industry standard, organization standard, previous result, or any other standard that will help you determine the difference between the measured data and the desired state. This difference can be expressed in a simple result obtained by subtracting one figure from the other. You can also express the difference as a percentage so you can see the relative amount of the difference. Information can be calculated by hand, but is typically generated in spreadsheets where the calculations are much quicker and more variations of calculations can be done very quickly. Too many presenters stop at the information stage. They do the comparison and figure that is all they have to do, the audience will figure out what it means. That is a view that results in confusion for too many audiences. Without moving to the third stage of analysis, as a presenter you have shortchanged your audience.

Insight

What your audience is looking for is insight into what the numbers mean to them. Insight requires reflection and may require you to take a broader view of the information along with other information to determine what it means to this audience. Audiences won't do the work to figure out what the numbers mean. They will leave confused and not be able to use what you have presented. They are expecting you to have done the thinking to come up with the insights that will help them make better decisions, use the information to improve their work and lives, or be better informed for the future.

For example, if we measure the number of transactions this month, we might find that it is 62. On its own, this is just data. The number, 62, doesn't mean anything until we turn it in to information. When we compare the measured value of 62 against the organization's goal of 60, we now have information that shows we are above what was expected. While this is an accurate calculation, it does not tell us what we should do about this measured value. We take it to the next stage by looking at what this number means. We may look at a trend to see that while we are above the goal, this is a continuation of a downward trend that started six months ago. In this case, we want to highlight the trend and recommend that the executives take action because the trend suggests that next month we will not meet the goal. In this example you can see that at the data and information stages, the audience would not be provided with what they need in order to make a good decision. It isn't until you take it to the next step and share the insight that puts the number in context and allows the executives to make an informed decision about what they should do in the future.

Strategy 4: Eliminate data that is not relevant

It may be convenient to just include a few extra rows or columns of numbers, or a few extra lines or columns on a graph because the data is there anyway. While this is taking the easy way out as a presenter, it causes confusion in the audience and it ultimately does not help the audience reach the goal of the presentation. Just because you have the numbers doesn't mean you should use all of them in your presentation. Carefully select the specific numbers you need to make your point. Eliminate any numbers that are not directly related to your point. If you are showing the results of a calculation, don't show each intermediate number, just show the results. For example, if you are showing the financial results for the quarter compared to last quarter, you don't need to show the figure for last quarter, the figure for this quarter, the raw difference, and the difference expressed as a percentage. The audience only wants to know the percentage difference, because that is what tells them the relative performance. You can reduce the numbers on the slide by 75%.

Another aspect of data that is not relevant is the level of precision we show when displaying numbers. A spreadsheet will calculate numbers to an almost infinite number of decimal places. Just because the calculations can be done this way doesn't mean we should show a large number of decimal places on a slide. Using that level of numerical precision doesn't make the number easier to understand. Most people prefer no more than one decimal place when looking at numbers. Keep it simple and eliminate the further precision that is not relevant to understanding the point you are making.

Strategy 5: One main point or idea per slide

Information overload also happens when a presenter tries to pack too many points on one slide. The audience gets confused trying to figure out how the points relate to each other. I suggest that you make each slide only about one point. If you have more than one point you want to cover, create another slide for that second point. When I give this suggestion in my workshops, people ask whether that will increase the total number of slides in their presentation. It likely will, but I don't see that as an issue. In the past, you may have heard of certain "rules" about how many slides you should have for a presentation of a specific length. Those so called "rules" don't apply today. When all you had were text overheads, there may have been some usefulness to some of those guidelines, but not anymore. With the use of visuals, a slide might be up for a few seconds and it might be up for a few minutes. The only guideline I suggest is to use as many or as few slides as you need to effectively communicate your message.

If you have related points, I suggest that you introduce the group of points with a context setting slide so the audience knows how they are related, then you can discuss the details of each point on its own slide. For example, if you want to talk about three aspects of preparing your home for sale, don't pack all of the details of each one on a single slide. Start with a slide that introduces the three aspects and how they relate to each other. Then you can show a detailed slide for each aspect. You end up with four slides, but the message is much easier for the audience to understand.

Information overload is the single biggest issue that presenters need to address in presentations. Use the five strategies in this chapter: the questioning strategy, the three R's of focusing your point, moving from data to information to insight, eliminating data that is not relevant, and one main point per slide to focus the content of your presentation.

CHAPTER SEVEN

D – Detailed Plan For Each Slide

It is important to separate the thinking about what each slide should contain from the mechanics of creating the slide in software. Planning your slide on paper first allows you to focus on the best way to communicate the point without being distracted by the software. After you have a plan, you can create the slide in the software. It can be very helpful to plan each slide on a sticky note or a half-page form as shown below.

Headline: Slide #:
Sketch of visual:
Data source:
Additional information:

Creating an effective slide is the topic of Chapters 10 to 21, so I will give you an overview of each section of the slide plan here and more details will follow in those chapters.

At the top of each slide you should write a headline that summarizes the message you want the audience to remember about this point. You can use the detailed outline of content you created before to give you guidance on what these headlines should be. The body of the slide should be a visual that illustrates the point you are making. While many presenters think that you have to have some graphic talent or design skills in order to create effective visuals, I will show you in Chapters 12 to 18 that any presenter can create visuals that are effective. Use the advice and examples in those chapters to determine the best visual for the point you are trying to make. Once you have decided on the visual, sketch it on your slide plan. Sketching the visual is a great way to see what you are thinking and verify that the visual will work for the point you are making.

In order to speed the slide creation process, the next section of the detailed slide plan is recording where the data or information will come from when creating the slide. It may be a report that needs to be run, certain columns from a spreadsheet, or interviewing a key customer. By deciding on the source now, you make it easy to get others involved in creating some of the slides. They will know exactly where to go to get the required information. The last part of the slide plan is to note any instructions around delivery of the slide, such as build sequence or links to other slides or exterior files. This helps you keep track of elements that will impact how the slide is delivered.

Some presenters find it helpful at this point to also jot down some speaking notes to help them remember key points they want to emphasize on each slide. I usually don't find this necessary if each slide has only one point summarized by a good headline at the top of the slide. But if this presentation will be delivered by someone else, or you fear that you might forget the great ideas you had while creating the slide plan, by all means add any speaking notes you feel are necessary.

CHAPTER EIGHT

S – Sufficiently Prepared To Present

Creating a clear message and persuasive slides is not enough to ensure that your presentation is effective. You need to prepare for the delivery of the presentation. This includes practicing and rehearsing the presentation. It also includes making sure you have everything you will need for the presentation, setting up early for the presentation, and being prepared to handle any potential issues. When you are delivering the presentation, use the best practices from professional speakers for in-person and web-based presentations. This chapter covers all of these topics so you are prepared to present your presentation.

Practice and Rehearse

Presenters need to be sufficiently prepared in order to deliver confidently. Too often a presenter thinks they can just "wing it", but that approach rarely results in an effective presentation. I suggest you practice and rehearse your presentation. Practice and rehearsal are two different activities.

Practice is running through your presentation silently, in your mind. You may advance through your slides, thinking through what you plan to say; check you have the right speaking notes, and become more comfortable with the sequence of the points. Practice is important, but it is not sufficient. You also need to rehearse, which is standing and delivering your presentation out loud, as if you are in front of the audience.

Rehearsing is the only way to make sure what you planned to say comes out properly and flows well. It also allows you to make sure that your presentation will fit into the time allotted to you. When I ask if people like it when the presenter runs over the allotted time, no one puts their hand up. So why does it happen so often? Because the presenter has never rehearsed, and is "rehearsing live." If you can rehearse in the room you will be delivering in, you can also become familiar with the equipment you will be using. Both practice and rehearsal help prepare you to confidently deliver your presentation.

Preparation before you leave for the presentation

What to Test in Advance

What do you think when you see a presenter with spelling errors on their slides, linked files that don't work, or images that appear blurry? Like me, you probably start to lose interest, or think less highly of the presenter and their message. You can reduce the probability of these types of problems happening in your presentation by checking the following at the office and in the meeting room 30 to 60 minutes before you begin to speak:

- Check the spelling on each slide by reading the words in reverse order and getting someone else to read the slides for you.

- Check the grammar on each slide by reading the words out loud and making sure the order and punctuation sound correct.

- Run through the animation sequence to make sure everything appears when it is supposed to.

- Activate every hyperlink and make sure that it works properly.

- Play every audio and video clip to make sure it plays and the volume is audible.

- Check all projected images to make sure they look crisp and clear when shown on a large screen.

- Check all special symbols that you have used to make sure that the operating system and PowerPoint version are still displaying the correct symbol.

By checking these items before you present, you are more assured that the presentation will run smoothly.

Equipment checklist

Before you leave to deliver your presentation, whether it is down the hall or across the country, make sure you have everything you will need. The following list will be helpful in remembering the equipment and information to bring with you.

Laptop/Tablet equipment: While it is obvious to remember your laptop or tablet, the power adapter is one item that presenters sometimes forget. Make sure you have the right power cords and adapters for the laptop or tablet you will be using. I also suggest that you use a presentation remote to advance your slides. Pack the remote and the receiver in your computer bag. If your presentation remote runs on batteries, also throw a spare set of batteries in your bag, just in case you need them.

Data projector/Flat screen TV monitor: Check with the venue and organizer to see if you need to bring a projector, they will provide one, or you will be presenting on a flat screen TV monitor. If you are bringing a projector, make sure you have all of the pieces you need: the projector, power cables, and video cables or adapters. Consider whether you will connect your laptop or tablet to the projector or monitor through a VGA or an HDMI cable and bring the correct cable and adapter if necessary. Also ask if you need to bring a screen to project on to. If this is a presentation where you are travelling, it may be easier to rent this equipment from a local source instead of carrying your own.

Audio equipment: If your presentation contains audio from either a sound file or audio associated with a video, you will need a way for the audience to hear it clearly. Laptop speakers are usually not sufficient because they are directed towards the presenter, not the audience, and they are usually not powerful enough to fill the room. So you will want to carry a speaker with you. For small to medium sized rooms, you can probably use one of the mini speakers that are available for portable music players. They are very small, but output big sound. Make sure you have any power cords and audio connection cords that the speakers may need (some connect to a headphone jack and some connect to a USB port). Even if the speaker has a rechargeable battery, bring the power adapter just in case. If you are in a larger room or using a more sophisticated setup, you may need an adapter from the headphone jack on your computer to the audio system in the room. Ask if you need to bring this and what one the venue or AV Company recommends.

Microphone equipment: For larger venues, you will likely be using a microphone. In most cases they will supply this equipment, but some presenters own their own microphones and prefer to use what they are familiar and comfortable with. If you are bringing your own microphone, make sure you pack all the pieces and cords, along with spare batteries if it is a wireless device. If you are also bringing the sound system, make sure you have the speakers, mixing board, and all cables.

Power cables: It may not seem like you have to be concerned with power, but I have found that this is one area that is important to think about. I often bring an extension cord with me when I speak. I don't know why, but power outlets in so many rooms are not placed in a spot that makes it easy to connect our equipment. By bringing an extension cord, I ensure that I can have the power where I need it to be. I also carry a surge protecting power bar. Not only does it give me enough outlets for all of my equipment, but it also protects the equipment from power surges, which are a reality in industrial venues, less developed countries, and anywhere during thunderstorms.

Required files/software: Make sure you have loaded all the software and files you will need on your presentation equipment. Copy all PowerPoint files, linked files, video files, audio files, and any other files you may need to access during or before the presentation. Make sure that the files can be successfully read on the device. If you are using a tablet, make sure that the files have been converted or uploaded to a service that puts them into a format that is useable on the tablet. If you are accessing a website live during the presentation, make sure that the browser on the device has the required plug-ins or add-ins to run the content you want to show. If your presentation does include live web access, I suggest you bring screen captures of the key web pages along as a backup. Internet access is notoriously poor in many conference rooms and you don't want to rely on access if it will let you down during the presentation. You can have these screen shots as hidden slides in your PowerPoint file so that you can quickly switch to them if you discover that Internet access is not available or not reliable.

Notes & logistics: Make sure you have your notes and any handouts you need for the audience. I suggest you bring these in both soft and hard copy formats, just in case. If you are having the handouts printed by an outside printer, make sure you check them over a day before your presentation. I have had the printer only print the first few pages of a handout for an all-day workshop. It left me scrambling to get the rest of the handout printed so we could complete the topics for the day. I also suggest you have a printout of all the slides you are using in the presentation. This can be four or six slides per page. This slide printout will be crucial if your technology fails and you have to create alternative visuals on the fly. At least you will know what you were planning to show. Bring whatever travel documents you require: confirmation of bookings, contracts, contact information for key people or venues, travel documents, maps, and other documents you may need. Create a checklist of these for your own situation, keeping in mind that international travel requires more documents than local travel.

Backups: Always have your key files backed up in case something happens to your equipment. All files should be copied to a USB flash drive that is kept in a different place than your equipment (so if your equipment is stolen, your backup is not). I also suggest you copy the files to a cloud based storage site so that the files can be accessed from any device if needed. Carry backups of your notes and handouts in case they need to be printed from source documents. I suggest these backups be in PDF format so that they will look the same regardless of what system you are using.

Preparing the room and equipment to present

Positioning the screen and equipment in the room

Different rooms and different circumstances will dictate how you will be able to set up the screen and equipment in the room. Some rooms have fixed screens and projectors, so you have no choice of where the equipment is set up. This is also the case in many conferences where the AV company has set up the room based on instructions from the organizers and the setup cannot be changed. If you do have a choice of where the screen is set up, I suggest that it be in the center of the front of the room. The projector can then display the image so it is easy for everyone to see it. You will stand to the left of the screen when looking at the screen from the audience's perspective. This is the preferred side to stand on. It is easier for people's eyes to come back to you on the left side after looking at the visual on the screen. In the Western world we read starting on the left and have a natural tendency to come back to that side with our eyes. Whether you are able to stand to the left of the screen or not, you want to make sure that you stand in an area that is not blocking the view of any audience member. Before your presentation, sit in the far left and far right seats in the first row and see where the sightlines are in those seats. Now you know where you will be able to stand and move during your presentation.

I also suggest keeping the barriers between you and the audience to a minimum. A podium or lectern is a physical barrier that separates you from the audience. If you need a place to put your notes or your laptop, I prefer a table that is not as high as a podium or lectern. It still allows you a spot for your materials, but is less imposing. You may need to do some rearranging of the stage or front of the room to accomplish a minimization of the barriers. I carry an extension cord for the video connection to the projector so that I can move my laptop away from barriers such as lecterns. Being closer to the audience allows for a better connection between presenter and audience members.

Lighting

The lighting in the room will impact how well the audience can see your slides and use the handouts you have given them. You need enough light for people to see the handout and write notes, but not too much light that it washes out the image on the screen. The ideal setup is to have the front of the room darker so that the screen image is bright, with the rest of the room well lit. You don't want the front totally dark, as then the audience won't be able to see you when you are presenting. If possible, turn off only the lights above the screen. You will want to work with the facility staff to see what is possible for lighting choices. Don't cover up lights with paper or other material, since it will create a fire hazard. Sometimes the facility staff will take a bulb or two out of a fixture if there is no switch that controls only the lights you need dimmed. Don't take bulbs out yourself, always ask a facility staff member to do it. If the screen is portable, the staff may also be able to move it a small amount to get the lights above to shine behind the screen instead of right on it. Because it may take some time to fix a lighting issue, it is a good idea to arrive an hour early if possible.

Starting equipment

While it has become easier to get the computer and projection equipment to connect since the first PowerPoint presentations were done, there is still an order that you should follow in order to have the best chance of a successful first connection. First, start the projector or flat screen TV. This allows the projector or TV to send a signal to the connected devices telling them it is on and its resolution. Turn on the audio system if you are using audio from the computer. Connect the video cable to the computer (VGA or HDMI) and the audio cable (usually to the headphone jack). Turn on the computer. Now, when the computer starts up, it will see the projector or TV and set the resolution to the appropriate setting. If the image is not projecting, it is likely due to either the resolution not being set properly or the computer not being in the proper display mode. Set the resolution of the computer to the default projector/ TV resolution and set the computer to display on both the computer screen and the projector/TV. For more solutions to setup problems, refer to the list of problems and solutions at **m.ThinkOutsideTheSlide.com**. After the computer is working with the projector or TV, you can plug in any remotes or mice that you are planning to use. Test that the slides look good when projected and the remote is working as expected. Now your technology is ready to go.

Your space (notes, water, etc.)

The final part of setting up for a successful presentation is setting up the space you will be presenting from. Determine where you will place your speaking notes so that you can see them easily and you have enough room to move them during the presentation. Practice how you will move from one page to the next during the presentation. I don't suggest you flip from one page to the next. I suggest you slide one page over to reveal the next page. It is easier for you as a presenter and less distracting for the audience. If you are using a tablet with notes in a word processing or PDF document, make sure it is easy to move from one page to the next and that the tablet will not go to sleep during the presentation (waking it up can be distracting to you and the audience).

You need to keep your throat hydrated during your presentation, so pour yourself a glass of water or get a bottle of water. Room temperature water is better than ice water as the cold restricts the power of your voice. Place the glass away from your electronic equipment so that a spill does not cause a disastrous accident. Feel free to take a sip of water during the presentation. When you are moving from one point to another is usually a natural spot to pause for a sip of water.

If you are using a microphone, connect with the audio support person and test the microphone. If it is a microphone that is attached to your clothing or ear, get it attached and know how to turn on the belt pack when it is time to present. If it is a wired microphone, know where you can walk within the limits of the length of the cord. To have a comfortable volume for your audience, know how far the mic should be from your mouth when using a handheld microphone. When using an attached mic, make sure it is turned off until right before you are to speak. You don't want private conversations or other sounds broadcasted to everyone in the room. When using a microphone, speak at a normal conversational volume level. Don't raise or lower the volume of your voice in an attempt to compensate for the use of a microphone. Let the equipment do its job while you do your job of presenting.

Preparing to handle problems during the presentation

Adjusting the length of your presentation

It has happened to almost every presenter at one time in their career: you have prepared a 45-minute presentation, and now they want it delivered in less time because other parts of the meeting ran late. What should you do? One thing you should not do is to try to rush through all of your slides to fit everything into the shorter timeframe. The audience will leave feeling like they were drinking from a fire hose and will not be able to retain anything you said.

Refer to the presentation outline that you created and you will know what the key points are that you need to make. To shorten your presentation, first cut out some of the supporting information that you can briefly speak to instead of cover in detail. Whenever you are cutting slides from your presentation, never delete the slide, simply hide it so that the slide is still in the file and can be accessed during the presentation if needed (use the technique for jumping to any slide described later in this chapter).

If you still need to shorten your presentation, cut one or two of the key points or combine key points if possible. Make sure to cover the points verbally, but don't have a separate slide if your time has to be drastically reduced. I once reduced a planned 12-minute presentation down to one slide when I was introduced a full thirty minutes after the meeting was supposed to have ended. By staying true to your outline, you can still have a strong message in a shorter timeframe.

Offer to send the participants the full set of slides for their reference if you feel it would provide a good follow up to the briefer presentation you delivered. Unhide the slides you cut before sending the presentation to them.

Have a backup plan

It is inevitable that something will go wrong at some point during one of your presentations. While the technology has become much more reliable over the years, it is not perfect. So you need to have a backup plan thought through in advance. One of the key components of your backup plan is to also have your presentation saved somewhere other than your computer. You can use a portable media such as a USB or flash drive, which allows you to plug in to another computer and continue with your presentation. You can also put a copy of your presentation on a web accessible storage space. This is a little harder to use during a presentation as you would need to access the web and download the file in order to start presenting again. Some presenters prefer to store the file on their phone or tablet. These devices can act as a portable drive or some can even allow you to present directly from the device, acting as a dual purpose backup. Whatever strategy works best for you, make sure your presentation file and all associated linked files or media are saved to another spot so you can access them in case your system fails shortly before or during the presentation.

Your backup plan also should include how you will proceed if the technology does not work anymore. Sometimes having backups will not help since the problem is not always something that can be fixed quickly. In this case, you will have to proceed without any technology. Make sure you have your speaking notes easily accessible so that you can still present the points you need the audience to hear. Draw key visuals using whatever non-technical equipment you have available, such as a blackboard, whiteboard, or flipchart. If you don't have a surface to draw on, you will have to draw in the air with your hands. Remember that you will need to draw so that it makes sense from the audience's point of view, which will be backwards from your perspective. As easy as it sounds, this is more difficult than you think it is and I suggest you practice ahead of time so that you can do it comfortably if you have to.

What to do when something goes wrong

It is important to think through what you will do when something goes wrong with the technology in your presentation. Notice how I said "when" and not "if." That is because it is inevitable that at some point in time, your technology will fail. I have had my laptop permanently fail during a presentation (the motherboard died), the software freeze up, the laptop screen blow just before I started, and a projector that had one color spectrum fail before the presentation. When it happens to you, what should you do?

First, stay composed and in control. If you are at a venue that has an AV or tech support person available, ask them to help fix the problem while you continue your presentation. If you have to solve the problem yourself, ask the audience to do a short exercise or discussion based on what you have already presented, or call a short break if it is a longer session. The audience feels for you and their first thought will be, "I am so glad that isn't me at the front of the room." Audiences tell me that the presenter has about 3-4 minutes to fix the problem, or abandon the technology and continue without it. Remember that the audience expects you to continue because they want to hear the rest of what you have to say. The most common steps you can take to get the technology going again include restarting each piece of equipment, and checking that all the cables are properly attached and haven't become loose or disconnected. If there is no obvious solution or the problem recurs after restarting the equipment, it is likely time to abandon your slides. You will use your speaking notes to guide what you want to say and you will use the techniques described earlier to create visuals for the audience.

Delivery Tips

Face the Audience, not the Screen When Presenting

What is more important when you are presenting, looking at the screen or looking at the audience? Obviously looking at the audience. So why do so many presenters look at the screen when they present? Whether it is nerves or habit, it doesn't make for an effective presentation. What should you do instead? Here are some suggestions.

First, position the laptop so you can see the laptop screen from where you will be standing when you present. If you need to glance at the screen to see what the next point is, glance at the laptop screen instead of turning around to the screen on the wall. If you can't position the laptop so you can see it from where you are standing, turn your head briefly so you can see the screen, turn back so you face the audience, and then begin speaking. Don't speak while you are facing the screen.

Second, if you are relying on the slides as speaking notes, you need to rehearse more and you should start using more effective slides. By rehearsing more, you will be more comfortable with the material and you will not need to constantly be looking at the screen to remind yourself what to say. By using more effective slides, it forces you to stop relying on text notes and start telling the story that explains the graph, diagram, or other visual, which is a more effective way of presenting.

Third, if you are facing the screen because you are nervous about facing the audience, you need to become more comfortable with speaking and presenting. Join a local Toastmasters group or attend a public speaking course that can help you become comfortable speaking in front of an audience.

Videotape yourself presenting or have a trusted colleague watch to see if you are facing the screen when speaking. If you are, use these ideas to break this habit and start connecting better with your audience.

Jumping to any Slide During Your Presentation

Most PowerPoint presentations will be delivered in a linear manner, starting at slide one and proceeding to the last slide. If an audience member asks a question or you want to move to another part of the presentation part way through, you can jump to any slide in your file using one of two techniques.

First, if you know the slide number you want to jump to, simply enter that number using the numeric keys on the keyboard and press the "Enter" key. This jumps to that slide without the audience seeing the slides that were skipped over. This is useful if you know the slide number of your conclusion slide and need to jump straight to it because of time constraints. It is also useful when you want to display a prepared slide that you have saved in case a certain question gets asked. Jump to the prepared slide to answer the question; then jump back to the slide you were on.

The second method is not as seamless as the first. In Slide Show mode, press Ctrl+S to bring up a list of all the slides in the file. It lists the slide number and the title of the slide if there is one. Any hidden slides will have their slide number in brackets. You can select any slide in the list, including a hidden slide, and click the "Go To" button to jump to that slide. The audience will see you do this, but it will be acceptable if they have specifically asked you to go to that slide and they will appreciate your flexibility in presenting what they want to see at that moment. When you want to return to where you were in the presentation, use the same steps to select the slide you were on before jumping to the requested slide. The dialog box will list the slide you were on before, making it easier to select the slide to go back to.

Drawing on the Slide in PowerPoint

Before PowerPoint was popular, a common visual aid was the overhead transparency. You could display a pre-printed transparency, and you could also write on it, or even use a blank sheet and create your own visual by drawing on it. Many presenters would like to be able to write on their slides sometimes to illustrate a point. You can do this in PowerPoint. Here's how to draw on your slide in Slide Show mode.

1. Press Ctrl+P (hold the Control key and press the P key) to turn the cursor into a pen cursor. You can right-click and select pen options, such as type of pen, color of ink, and thickness of line.

2. Use your left mouse button to draw on the slide as you would in a drawing program. This is usually easier to do with a mouse than with the trackpad on a laptop. It also takes practice to make the drawing look smooth. Some presenters prefer a drawing tablet or a touchscreen laptop instead of a mouse to give better control.

3. If you want to erase a portion of the drawing, press Ctrl+E to change the cursor to an eraser cursor. This eraser removes entire lines, not portions of lines, so be careful using it and practice before you present. Press Ctrl+P to change back to the pen cursor. If you want to erase everything you have drawn, press the E key.

4. When you are done drawing, press Ctrl+A to return to the regular cursor, and press A to hide the cursor. When you exit Slide Show mode, the program will ask if you would like to save what you have drawn on the slides. This can be helpful if you are capturing input or

discussions with the audience and want to have the drawings for distributing to others after the presentation is over. The drawings get saved as simple line objects on your slides and can be edited later.

Drawing on your slides is not something that you will do in every presentation, but it is good to know that you can if you need to. It increases the effectiveness of your message when you can customize a slide or capture ideas without disrupting the flow of your presentation. Practice this technique if you are planning to use it in a presentation so that you can be comfortable drawing on a slide.

When to Turn off the Slides

Don't feel that just because you have selected to use slides for this presentation, that you always need a slide on the screen at all times. There are times during your presentation where you won't want a slide on the screen, such as when you want to share a story, engage the group in discussion, or answer a question that has been asked. In these situations, you will want to use a black slide so that the focus of the audience is only on you and they have no visual on the screen distracting them. If you know that you will be telling a story or you have a planned discussion time, create a black slide in your presentation by inserting a new slide and drawing a black rectangle that covers the entire slide. When you advance to this slide in your presentation, the audience will immediately look at you since there is nothing else to look at.

You can also go to a black screen at any time during your presentation. If someone asks a question and the visual on the screen is not relevant in answering the question, turn the slides off by pressing the period key (.) on your keyboard. This toggles the slides off and on. To display the slides again, press the period key once more. When the slides are turned off, the audience only pays attention to you and the answer you are giving. When you are ready to proceed with the rest of the presentation, turn the slides back on.

Giving yourself permission to turn the slides off can make a world of difference in the way you present. You know that you don't have to compete with the screen during those times in the presentation where you want the focus to be on you and what you are sharing.

Best Practices for Delivering Web-based Presentations

If you haven't delivered a presentation using a Web-conferencing service, you will soon. Travel budgets are being cut, and you will be holding more meetings virtually instead of in person.

If your organization does not have a standard Web-meeting service provider, you will need to select one from the many that exist. Here are some criteria to use when looking for a Web-meeting service provider:

1. Select a service that supports a variety of platforms, including both Windows and Mac computers. Some of your audience members may be accessing the service from home, and they won't be using the organizational standard hardware you are used to. With more people using tablet computers instead of laptops, see if the software supports the common mobile platforms as well.

2. Select a service that allows you to share your desktop instead of restricting you to content that you upload in advance. If you upload your slides, the service will convert them, sometimes resulting in changes to how the slides will appear during the presentation. Sharing your desktop increases your flexibility and makes your presentation more effective.

3. If possible, use a service that provides audio connections via either telephone line, or through the microphone and speakers on the computer. Give your audience members flexibility in the way they access the audio portion of the presentation.

4. Make sure that audio mute is available on both your end and the participant end. In noisy locations, such as an office, airport, or busy home, being able to mute an audio line makes the presentation better for everyone.

5. Use a service that allows you to switch presenters during the presentation. It allows you to include others in delivering the information. It even allows you to pass control to a participant who wants to show a particular issue or situation on their own PC, so that everyone can discuss it and help.

6. Match your intended usage to the pricing structure of the service. Some services are free, but offer limited features. Some services charge per participant per minute that they are connected. And some services charge a flat monthly fee. Find a service that will match your intended usage pattern the best.

There are many services available. This list of criteria will allow you to narrow down your choices to the one or two services that best meet your needs. Selecting the right service will help you make your Web-based presentations more effective.

A presentation you would give in person won't always work well when delivered over the Web. Here are some changes you should consider when designing presentations that will be delivered over the Web.

Eliminate movement effects: While Web conferencing has come a long way technically, one of the functions it doesn't handle well is movement of objects on the screen. Those moving arrows or fancy transitions between slides will look jerky, and the whole point of the movement will be lost when delivered over a Web-conferencing service. The hesitation in the movement is created by the delay in transmitting what is happening on your screen to all the participants. Cut out the movement and use simple animations, such as items simply appearing on the slide, or the next slide appearing in place without movement to get there.

Don't show video clips: One of the hottest trends in presentations is to use videos. Unfortunately, when presenting over the Web, video streaming doesn't work well. Most videos shown on the Internet are not streamed in real time like a presentation is. They are downloaded to your computer and played locally. Instead of having your video show poorly, convert that slide to a picture of the person speaking and the most important quote they make in the video. If you want the audience to view the video after the presentation, post it on your website or a video sharing site and direct them to it with an e-mail link following your presentation.

Use callouts to direct attention on visuals: If you would normally point to a spot on the slide in a live presentation, your audience on the Web won't be able to see where you are pointing. Use a callout as explained in Chapter 19. Adding callouts is also essential if you send a copy of your presentation to those who could not attend the presentation.

Design interactivity to keep their attention: In a live presentation, you can get feedback by looking at the audience's faces and body language. You lose that opportunity for feedback and interaction with a Web presentation. So you must design interaction for your Web-based presentation. Keep the audio line open, so you can hear them and include open ended questions that probe their thoughts on a topic, their experiences with an issue, or how they would answer a particular question. This interaction keeps them paying attention and not surfing the Web or checking e-mails.

Once you have designed your slides for delivery through a Web-based service, there are also some items you need to keep in mind so that the delivery goes smoothly. Here are some best practices when delivering Web-based presentations.

Use a second PC as a participant: No matter how fast your Web connection is, or how fast the connection of each participant is, there will always be a slight delay between when you show the next slide and when they see the slide on their screen. By the time the service takes your new slide, transmits it to the system's server, and then sends it out to each participant, anywhere from one to several seconds will elapse. The challenge is that you will not know when the participants are seeing the new slide unless you set up a second PC on your desk and connect that PC as a participant. Then you can advance to the next slide and keep transitioning with what you are saying until you see the new slide on the "participant PC." This way, your speaking can always match the visuals that your participants are seeing.

Use a standard screen resolution: Many computers today come with high-resolution monitors that can be quite large. Even laptops have wide screens that can show full HD resolution videos. But in almost all cases, the higher resolution will hurt instead of help your presentation. A 1680 by 1050 widescreen monitor has almost 2.25 times as many pixels as a normal XGA resolution of 1024 by 768 (which is the resolution of most projectors). That means that the Web-conferencing service will have to send more than twice as much data each time (2.25 times from your computer to the server and 2.25 times from the server to the participant). This means much slower load times for each slide and longer waits for the participants to see the next slide. And what if the participant doesn't have a high-enough resolution on their screen? Your well-designed visual may appear distorted or not even appear at all. It is best to reduce the resolution of your screen to 1024 by 768 (or something similar), so that the slides appear more quickly and look crisp on each participant's screen. You can always change the resolution of your computer back to the normal setting after the Web meeting is done.

Use callouts instead of drawing tools: One feature that the Web-meeting services offer is the ability to use drawing tools during your presentation. Most of the services allow the presenter to grab a virtual pen or highlighter and draw on the screen. While this may sound like it would be a great idea, be careful. Movement is very hard to show smoothly during Web meetings. Too often your drawing of a circle around an important concept or highlighting a key phrase will look jerky to the participants. This jerkiness makes the participants think that something isn't working properly or they missed something – both distract the participant from your message. Instead of using the drawing tools, create proper callouts that direct the attention to the important spot on the slide.

As you start to replace in-person presentations with Web presentations, keep these best practices in mind. You will find the presentations more effective and you will reach your objectives faster.

CHAPTER NINE

Applying The RAPIDS Approach
To Common Presentations

In the work that I do, I have determined there are four types of presentations that constitute the majority of presentations delivered. In order to help you in applying the RAPIDS approach to your presentations, I want to give you examples of how the RAPIDS approach would apply to each of the four common types of presentations. Use these examples as a guideline when you plan each of your presentations.

Example #1: Training/Education Presentation

Real Goal

The goal for a training presentation needs to be very specific. The goal is not only to share knowledge. The goal should be for that knowledge to be understood and applied in the context of the audience. Without understanding and application, a training presentation will not be successful. Your goal should state how the audience will use the information. This makes the destination of the presentation clear.

Audience Analysis

Keep in mind the following:

- The amount that the audience already knows about this topic. Aim the information so that it meets the knowledge level of the audience.

- The literacy level of the audience. If there is a low literacy level, use more pictures and visuals.

- What role in the process does the audience have? Do they need detailed information because they are front-line employees, or do they need more strategic viewpoints appropriate for a management level?

- What are the objections or areas of skepticism that the audience has about this topic? Make sure you address these in the presentation.

- Consider whether the information applies universally, or are there differences in how it applies in one jurisdiction compared to another.

- What role do you have as related to the information that is being discussed? If you were very involved in developing this area, you will have more credibility, especially when there are questions.

Presentation Outline

Creating the presentation outline, with the key points and supporting information, depends a lot on the audience analysis. Keep the following suggestions in mind when outlining a training presentation:

- Start with getting agreement from the group on the goal for the presentation. You can avoid wasting your time and theirs by making sure the audience is expecting the same topics to the same level of detail that you have prepared.

- Always include why any decisions were made regarding policies, rules, etc. People are more likely to accept new directions if they understand why the decisions were made.

- Make sure you relate the information to their situation. Use examples that relate to this group, and show them specifically what you want them to do with the information. As much as possible, illustrate the real-world application of the information so the audience sees why it is important to them.

- If you must show the audience the text of a rule/regulation/policy/procedure, don't just type the entire text on the screen and read it to them. Instead, include it in their handout, and refer them to the text. Give them time to read it to themselves. Then explain why it is important to them. If you need to show the text on the slide, highlight the key phrases and have them highlight those words in their handout. Follow any text slide with a visual that shows how this applies in their own situation (picture, video, screen capture, etc.) Textual information does not need to be a group reading exercise, it can be engaging.

- Build in time for participants to practice applying the information in case studies or exercises. Have discussions afterwards to clarify any misunderstandings and correct any errors in interpretation.

- Leave time for questions from the audience, so they know if they have questions that they will be able to ask them at some point during the presentation.

Information that is laser-focused

The biggest challenge with training presentations is that the audience will be so overloaded by information that they won't know where to start applying it. Here are some suggestions when paring down the information in a training presentation:

- Summarize information and focus on the most important items that the audience needs to hear. If you need the audience to refer to more detailed information, send them some pre-reading to do, provide a reference document for them to use afterwards, or plan a series of sessions following the presentation to deal with specific situations or applications of the information.

- Avoid the temptation to provide every aspect and scenario. Select the most common applications of the information to focus on.

- When presenting analytical information, remember to focus on the insights instead of the data. Often, analytical information is used to provide proof or justification. The real proof is shown by going beyond the analytical information to the insight that it provides.

Many times this insight is what convinces the audience to apply the training information.

Detailed plan for each slide

When planning the slides you will use in a training presentation, it is important to keep in mind that you want the audience engaged in order to understand the information and be willing to apply it. This means that you should keep text slides to a minimum because too much text leads to reading the slides. Instead, use visuals such as diagrams to show a process; photos to show the actual location, product, or situation; videos that demonstrate what you are speaking about; graphs that show numeric information; and other types of visuals (you will see many examples of visuals in Chapters 13 to 18).

Sufficiently prepared to present

Many training presentations will be done more than once, as a new policy, new procedure, or new initiative is launched. After you have done your practice and rehearsal, make sure you do a pilot session with people who represent typical audience members to get feedback on the presentation. Take their feedback seriously and improve the presentation. If this is a large scale initiative with many sessions to be held, create checklists of equipment that the presenter will need for each session. Create a process so that the right materials and equipment are ready when needed. Plan and practice how to handle issues such as materials or equipment not arriving, technology failing during the session, or participants not being prepared for the session. Think through and plan for the challenges that will inevitably occur. Plan how you want the room set up and send a diagram with detailed instructions to the venue where the training will take place. After having done hundreds of training workshops, I can tell you from personal experience that a venue greatly appreciates a detailed list of setup instructions. As the presenter, arrive early to make sure all of the materials and equipment are there and set up, and the room is arranged as requested. Give yourself time to make any adjustments before the audience arrives. This ensures you are ready to greet the audience and make them feel welcome.

Example #2: Status/Update/Review/Briefing Presentation

This type of presentation is known by many different names, but essentially it is a presentation where we are updating an audience on what has been happening in our area of the organization or work that we have been assigned.

Real Goal

The biggest risk in this type of presentation is that the presenter does not understand the true goal of the presentation. The goal is not just to update the audience on what you have been doing. The goal is more important than a simple information sharing time. There are two goals that you should be considering. The first is to convince the group that the situation is in control, no changes need to be made, and the current work should continue to be supported. Too many presenters assume they still have the support of management and are surprised during the presentation when questions indicate support is wavering.

The second goal may be to ask the group for support to move in a slightly different direction or change the type of support (financial, personnel, timing) that is being given. I have seen too many project or functional managers come out of a meeting with their management team frustrated that they didn't get approval for changes. When I inquire about what happened, it becomes clear that the presenter never asked for approval of changes. The manager just assumed that the audience would know the goal of the presentation and didn't think they needed to be clear about it.

Depending on the situation you find yourself in, one of these two goals will likely focus your thoughts and message better than simply a list of what has been done in the past month. This is your opportunity to shore up support and raise your visibility to executives.

Audience Analysis

The audience for a status presentation can vary greatly and can significantly impact the content of the presentation. Consider the following when analyzing the audience for this type of presentation:

- Given that a decision about support must be made, it is critical to know who the decision makers are in the group and who are the influencers in the group. You will want to know as much as you can about these people, since they will have a significant impact on your ability to reach your goal. Consider what they have supported in the past or what is "hot" in the organization right now. Also consider whether their decision making process includes pre-reading so that they can become comfortable with a direction or change. If pre-reading is required, get the appropriate documents to them in plenty of time for them to review the information and develop a comfort with what you will be saying.

- If you are presenting to peers and not management, do not make the mistake of thinking that they are less important for these types of presentations. The support of peers is critical to your objective and, while less direct in nature, is still considered important by the decision makers. The information peers will need is different from decision makers, so plan your presentation accordingly.

- Try to find out the criteria used to decide on continued support of your work. The more you know about the criteria the individuals will be using, the better you can tailor your presentation to those needs. Different people will have slightly different criteria, so focus on the most commonly used criteria.

- The level of knowledge varies greatly between different groups for whom you may be presenting a status update. Peers in different areas may know a little about your work and are mainly interested in how it will impact their area or jobs. Management that have your work as a key deliverable on this year's plan, are personally vested in the project and will know more about the details. Your staff and those affected by your work are the most knowledgeable and will likely need more detail than other groups. Make sure you tailor your presentation to the correct level based on who is attending the presentation.

- Actively seek out the objections or concerns that the audience has about your work. You want to be prepared to address these during the presentation and not be blindsided by a concern or objection that is raised. Different groups will have different concerns, so don't necessarily use the same list for each presentation.

- If you are not known to the group you are presenting to, arrange to have someone they know and trust introduce you at the presentation. This gives you additional credibility with the group. If they aren't familiar with you, they may not trust what you say as much as they would from someone they know. You can get "third-party" credibility from having a trusted person introduce you.

Presentation Outline

Keep these ideas in mind as you develop your presentation outline:

- Always start with a summary of the key measurements that you know they are looking for and any requests you will have of them. They need the big picture first to put the rest of what you present in context. If there are problems, admit them up front. Don't try to bury them in the presentation hoping that the audience won't notice (they always do). This is not a mystery novel where you want to reveal the requests at the end. Executives don't like surprises, so saving the requests until the end makes them uncomfortable and they will likely end up delaying any decisions until they have had more time to think about them. By previewing the requests up front, they have time to consider the detailed information in each area within the context of the request and can be more confident making a decision at the end of the presentation.

- Present one idea at a time, checking for understanding and answering questions as you proceed. In order to build the case for support, you need to make sure that the audience is following your points and understands them. Build in pauses for questions and discussion so that the presentation is more of a conversation with the audience than a one-way lecture. By building agreement along the way, it is more likely that they will agree with the final conclusion at the end.

- It is unlikely that every update will be one where all aspects of your work are going exactly according to plan. It is likely that some areas will not be measuring up to expectations or standards. This is expected by the audience because they have a realistic view of the situation. What they will be looking for is what action plans you have to bring the performance back into line with the expectations. Be specific and explain how those actions will reverse the negative trend. If you believe that the deviation is simply a timing issue that will correct itself, make sure to explain when the performance will return to expected levels and how you will determine if the issue is something other than simply a timing issue.

- For certain audiences, you should be prepared to go deeper if they want to explore a specific point you are making. In this case, prepare the further details in hidden slides, or in source documents or spreadsheets. Create hyperlinks to these detailed slides or files from your presentation slides. Practice using the hyperlinks to access the detailed information, so that if the request comes during the presentation, you can smoothly answer the question by showing the detailed source information. The level of detail an audience needs depends on who is attending the presentation, so this is an area where you will have to consider the needs of each audience and prepare accordingly.

- If you have a situation where you can have a very free-flowing discussion with the audience and they may want to go in a number of potential directions, consider using a non-linear presentation. A non-linear presentation allows you to present the audience with a list of topics that you are prepared to discuss. You ask the audience which topics they consider a priority at that time and the sequence of the presentation is determined by their choices. This is a less formal presentation style, and can be very effective with certain audiences who may have a number of concerns.

Information that is laser-focused

Overloading the audience with information is a good way to confuse them and erode your support with this group. Tightly focus on what matters to this group and exclude other information that, while possibly interesting, is not what this audience needs in order to give support or make decisions. If you are presenting analysis in support of a request, only show the final result of your calculations, not all the steps in-between. The audience wants the insight you have gained from the analysis, they don't want to see all the details.

Detailed plan for each slide

When creating slides for your status update presentation, consider using visuals that will be easy for executives to understand. For schedules, consider time-based diagrams like a Gantt chart or calendar diagram. These diagrams visually show the time a task takes or shows when it will be completed. The timeline or calendar makes it easy to see how tasks relate to each other on the dimension of time. For budget discussions, don't just copy a spreadsheet onto a slide. Summarize the key figures and show a summary table, highlighting the key figures they need to pay attention to. Consider other diagrams or visuals that can help the executives quickly and easily understand your message. The better they understand, the easier it is for them to support you.

Sufficiently prepared to present

It is likely that you have presented to this audience in the past, since regular update presentations are common for many professionals. Just because you have presented similar information in the past, does not mean you can skip the preparation to present phase. Anticipate questions that you may be asked and practice answering them. If it will be helpful, create hidden slides in your PowerPoint file that you can jump to when answering these questions. Make sure you check on any changes to what the audience is anticipating or how their situation has changed, and what different information they may need or be expecting. If you are having a team member present part of the presentation, make sure they practice and rehearse. Also make sure that you have both practiced how you are going to switch presenters during the session (what you will say to pass the presentation from one to another, how you will hand the remote or control of the equipment to one another, where you will stand or sit, etc.)

Example #3: Sales Presentation

While some aspect of every presentation is convincing the audience of your point of view, a sales presentation is one where the primary focus is to get agreement from the audience on what you are proposing. Many presenters don't realize that they are really delivering a sales presentation, but any time you are trying to convince the audience of going in a certain direction, adopting a certain position, or buying in to a solution to a problem, you are doing a sales presentation.

Real Goal

In a sales presentation, deciding on the goal may actually be a hard exercise. It sounds like it should be easy – the goal is to have the audience buy what I am selling by the end of the presentation. But it is not always so clear cut. There are many situations where the presentation is to outline our capabilities in order to generate interest in future business. There is no current sale to be made. In these situations, the goal may be to convince the audience that we are able to solve their problem when they decide to seek a solution. I remember one client situation where this was exactly the case. We focused the presentation on showing the process the company uses to solve problems and on presenting case studies proving the solutions were beneficial. Less than one month after presenting to the leading firm in a specific beverage market, my client received an invitation to bid on a significant new project.

A sales presentation is doomed to failure if it does not answer the one question the audience absolutely needs to have answered. What the audience really wants to know is, "Can you solve the big, hairy, ugly problem we have?" Until you answer that question, they don't care about the rest of what you have to say. So describe the goal of your presentation in terms of how you will solve that problem.

Audience Analysis

The audience for a sales presentation typically contains the decision-makers and influencers. Consider the following when analyzing the audience for this type of presentation:

- As much as possible, find out who will be attending the presentation and what their role is in the decision. Some people are attending for a specific reason and the key decision-makers will be looking to those individuals for advice on certain parts of your solution. Others are influencers who play a more subtle role but can be very important in the discussions and ultimate decision. Consider the decision-making style of the group to see if the ultimate decision will be made by one person or is there a consensus approach where agreement will be reached amongst all participants.

- Try as best you can to determine what the criteria will be for the decision. Sometimes there is a published list of criteria with weighting assigned to each aspect, and sometimes it is far more subjective. You will want to know what the key players consider the most important criteria to be. In many cases, personal feelings influence how each option gets rated on an objective rating scale, so you can't discount personal opinions even if the criteria are public knowledge.

- For the key people attending your presentation, figure out what their hot buttons are. What gets them excited, and what are the typical objections they have to any solution. You may need to talk with others who have presented to this group or individuals in the audience. Ask what objections were raised, and what aspects got people enthusiastic. You will want to emphasize those items that will be looked on favourably and address objections before they get raised by the audience in the presentation.

- Some decision-makers like to see reports in advance because they like to take time to contemplate the decision before the presentation. If you have to present a document in advance, find out how long it should be, what format they like it in, what sections should be included, and how far in advance they would like it. This may force you to lock in parts of your presentation in advance, so it matches the document that was sent.

- Consider the level of knowledge that the audience has about the problem or issue that you are proposing to solve. If they don't have a deep level of knowledge, you may need to start the presentation by reviewing the significant impact of the problem in terms of cost, productivity, time, etc. If they don't see the issue as being worth solving, your solution may be rejected. Beware that some decision-makers and influencers may think they have more knowledge than they really do. Address this in subtle ways so as not to embarrass them in front of their subordinates, peers, or their boss.

- Determine whether there is a bias towards a certain type of solution for this problem. Review your past discussions with audience members and ask others in the organization for their input. If you are in a situation where you are competing with other solutions, you will want to know if they have shown a tendency to favour a competing viewpoint and understand what they find attractive about that solution. This can help you counter some of those arguments or find ways to leverage certain aspects to promote your solution.

Presentation Outline

When you outline your presentation, keep the results of your audience analysis close at hand, since the success of this type of presentation depends so much on the individuals in the audience. Keep these ideas in mind as you develop your presentation outline:

- Start by showing that you understand their problem. Demonstrate that you know how much that problem is costing them in dollars and reputation. Confirm with them the source and level of pain.

- Now that you have demonstrated you understand their pain, outline the solution you are providing and how it solves their problem. When presenting your solution, keep the following in mind:

  - Make sure you are clear on the options you considered and the criteria used to arrive at the conclusion you are recommending. You want to leave the impression that your analysis was thorough and all options were considered before reaching this conclusion. You want the decision criteria to be similar to what your audience analysis determined would be the likely criteria for the decision-makers. This way you leave little room for doubt about the process used.

  - Provide information that shows the methods used are credible and can be relied upon. You can use previous analysis that has shown to be sound, standards that external organizations have created and are relied upon by others, and other objective viewpoints supporting the validity of your analysis methods. This serves to disarm those who might want to discredit the conclusion by attacking the methods used to reach the conclusion.

  - Any solution that you propose will have risks. Don't shy away from them or avoid discussing them in your presentation. Be upfront about the risks, how likely they are to happen, and the impact they would have if they occurred. Explain what steps you will take to mitigate the risks, either by preventing them from happening or reducing the impact if they do occur. By being forthright in your presentation, you can show that you are being open and not hiding information from the decision-makers.

- It is important to focus on the benefits of the proposed solution, not just the features. A feature is something that is part of the solution. A benefit is why that feature matters to the organization and those impacted by the solution. Make sure to spend time in the presentation explaining how your solution will benefit not only those in the organization, but the decision-makers personally. Many decisions are made emotionally, so you need to show the individual impact in your presentation.

- Make sure to answer the "five W" questions in your presentation:

  - What is the solution.

  - Who will be implementing it, and who will be impacted.

  - Where the solution will come from, where it will be implemented, and where in the organization the impacts will be seen.

  - When the solution should be started, when it will be completed, and when the benefits will be seen.

- How the recommended solution will solve the identified problem, how the solution works, how the organization will be impacted, and how progress will be measured during implementation.

- Use case studies that show how you have solved similar problems for others in the past. Chapter 18 contains four steps to create effective case studies.

- Only after you have shown proof that you have solved these types of problems in the past should you start talking about your organization or department. And when you do talk about your team, it is not to brag about how great you are. When you include information about yourself and your team, it should focus on the skills, experience, expertise, capabilities, machinery, facilities, etc. that you will use to provide the specific solution to the problem. The audience only cares about what will help solve their problem.

- After presenting a clear understanding of their problem, a summary of your solution, proof that you have solved similar problems for others, and details of how you will bring your experience to solve their problem, you can ask for questions and have a discussion.

Information that is laser-focused

You need to explain any analysis that was done, but only to an appropriate level of detail. Do not make the mistake of thinking that you need to include every little step taken in the analysis or every piece of data used. The decision-makers need to feel comfortable with the methods used, but don't need all the details. If you have too much detail, it can lead to confusion and even more questions as they start to focus on insignificant details that may actually be out of context. Your presentation can get derailed with too much detail. Use the strategies described in Chapter 6 to focus the information you decide to include in the presentation. Remember that you can always have hidden backup slides in case a question gets asked.

Detailed plan for each slide

The most important part of each slide in a sales presentation is the headline. The headline is what you want the audience to remember from this slide. Make sure you write good headlines for each slide so that the audience takes away the key messages you want them to remember.

In a sales presentation, you will want to use a variety of visuals to illustrate your points. You may want photos, drawings, or diagrams to show a product, location, or design. A map is a good way to show geographic information. A table organizes criteria and how options measure against the criteria. A diagram can show a process or information flow. In Chapters 13 to 18, you will see many ideas for effective slides.

Sufficiently prepared to present

A sales presentation is one of the most important presentations that you will deliver. For the best probability of having a successful presentation, practice and rehearse multiple times until you are totally comfortable with the presentation.

Have others watch and give you feedback to improve the presentation. Use the list described in Chapter 8 to make sure you have all the equipment and notes required to deliver the best presentation you can. Arrive early and be ready to go – don't rush in at the last moment and be flustered. Not every sales presentation will result in success, but if you are well prepared, you give yourself the best possible chance.

Example #4: Presenting a Recommendation

Presenting a recommendation is similar in many ways to a sales presentation because you are trying to convince an audience of decision-makers. A sales presentation is usually driven from the presenter's desire to make the sale, and the presenter and audience are often not from the same organization. A recommendation presentation is usually requested by the audience. They want the presenter to investigate possible solutions to a particular problem and present a recommended solution. The presenter and audience are often from the same organization. The differences in who is driving the request for the presentation and the relationship of the presenter to the audience impact how you structure and deliver a recommendation presentation compared to a sales presentation.

Real Goal

The goal when presenting a recommendation is quite straightforward. You want the decision-makers to accept and act on your recommendation. Don't make the goal too complex or you will lose focus.

Audience Analysis

Analyzing the audience when presenting a recommendation is very similar to the analysis you would do for a sales presentation. Refer to the Audience Analysis section for sales presentations earlier in this chapter for tips on:

- Roles of the different audience members

- The criteria used to make the decision

- The hot buttons and objections of the audience

- The expectations for materials in advance

- The level of knowledge and biases of the audience

Presentation Outline

The individuals in the audience and the details of their request to you are valuable inputs when planning the content of your presentation. Here are some ideas on structuring the presentation of a recommendation:

- Start with the recommendation itself. Decision makers don't want this to be a mystery novel where you reveal the recommendation at the end. If you want them to take action, you need to give them time to think and get comfortable with your conclusion. You can start by explaining what your recommendation is and that in the presentation you will explain how you came to that conclusion.

- In making your decision between the different options, you will have used some criteria in order to rank the options against each other. Review the criteria used to come to the recommendation. Explain how each of the criteria is relevant to the decision. Explain whether any criteria had greater weight in the decision and how weighting the criteria helped make a better decision between the options. Get agreement from the decision makers that the criteria and weightings are reasonable for making this decision.

- Next, discuss which options or possible solutions were in the short list you considered. Give a short description of each possible solution in case some are not familiar with each one. Consider whether you want to get agreement from the decision makers that the options on the short list are the correct ones. This is not always necessary or advisable since the decision makers may not be as familiar with the options that are available and may introduce unnecessary discussions at this point.

- Now that you have explained the criteria and the options, you can show how each option was evaluated against the criteria. I suggest you discuss the evaluation of each option separately so that you can focus the audience on the conclusions you reached for that option. Your recommended option will be the one that was evaluated as the best possible solution using the criteria discussed.

- Once you have shown how you arrived at the recommendation, it is time to ask for the decision. Don't think that just because your analysis has been solid that the audience will know you are asking for their decision. Don't assume they know what you want them to do. Ask them to approve the recommendation. It is at this point that they will have a discussion with you to confirm any concerns they have and ask any questions about your work. You should leave with an agreed action plan, even if it is to look at a few more items before final approval is given.

Information that is laser-focused

The one mistake too many presenters make when presenting a recommendation is to think that the audience wants to see everything you did to come up with the recommendation. They don't need to see all the analysis. They need to see the conclusions you drew from that analysis, but not all the details. Focus your analysis on answering the question, "What conclusion can I draw from the research, calculations, and thinking that has been done?"

The strategies in Chapter 6 will help you focus the information you include in your presentation. Hidden slides are a great way to prepare for questions or concerns you think the audience may raise.

Detailed plan for each slide

The most important slide in the presentation will likely be the one showing how each option measures up against the criteria you used. I suggest you use a comparison table to show this all in one slide. The table has the criteria in the left-most column. Then you have one column for each option considered. The column shows how that option measured up on the criteria listed in the first column. There may be some measurements that are numeric, in which case the number should go in that cell of the table. If it is more of a yes/no evaluation for a criteria, consider using a checkmark to indicate that the option met the criteria and leave the cell blank if the option did not meet the criteria. This makes it easier to see where an option did not meet some criteria because the blank cells stand out.

I suggest you build this table one option at a time so you have an opportunity to discuss the measurements with the decision makers. If you put all the columns on at the start, you will find it hard to focus the audience because they will be trying to interpret the whole table and won't be listening to your discussion of each option. Some people say that you should save the recommended option for the last column. This is not as much of an issue if you started the presentation by letting them know what the recommendation was already. Order the options in a way that makes sense so the audience sees your analysis as logical and supportive of the recommendation. Chapter 16 will give you more tips on creating comparison tables.

Sufficiently prepared to present

Because a recommendation presentation is usually an internal presentation, it will likely be more interactive than a sales presentation. You need to practice and rehearse so you are comfortable with the presentation. You also need to be prepared for more discussion with the audience than a typical sales presentation. Allocate a sufficient amount of the time you have been given for discussion and questions. Be prepared to go into more detail if asked. You may want to prepare hidden slides and practice accessing them from different places in the presentation so you can smoothly handle questions. The decision-makers won't always accept your recommendation, but preparing this type of presentation well will show your skills and raise your profile in the organization.

Section Three:

Creating Effective Slides

Introduction

When should you use a slide? There are two circumstances in which a slide will help communicate your message. First, when you want to illustrate your point with a visual, such as a graph, diagram, or photo. The visual in this case speaks volumes more than your words can, and it helps the audience understand your message more easily.

The second circumstance for choosing to use a slide is to guide the audience through a numbered list, bullet points, or a simple text list. The text points on the slide serve as a helpful visual reminder for the audience as you discuss each point.

Slides should never be used for speaker notes. I have nothing against speaker notes and in fact almost always use them myself. If you need some notes to remind yourself of what you want to say, then create notes on cards, sheets of paper, or a tablet computer to refer to as you speak. Disregard any commentators who try to say that you should never use notes when you speak. Rehearsing your presentation does not mean having it memorized, it is to be familiar with the topics and flow. In fact, sometimes during rehearsal you discover some additional points you want to include in your notes to ensure you share those points with the audience. Speaker notes are fine, they just don't belong on slides.

What does an effective slide look like? As I suggested in Chapter 7 on creating a detailed plan for each slide, an effective slide has a headline and a visual. You don't have to be a designer or have graphics training to create effective slides. In the following twelve chapters I will share basic guidelines for slide design, methods for creating effective headlines, techniques for selecting a visual to use, and examples of different visuals along with the best practices for creating them. You will soon be able to consistently create more effective slides.

CHAPTER TEN

Slide Design

The overall design of your slides should focus the audience on the points you are making. If the design makes the slide hard to read or distracting, the presentation will be less effective. Here are some guidelines to use when designing the look of your slides.

Choose Colors that Have Enough Contrast

Contrast is a measure of how different two colors are, and it determines how easy it is to see one color when placed on top of or beside the other color. If the colors do not have enough contrast, the audience can't tell the difference between the colors. If it is text, they won't be able to read it. If it is in a pie chart, they won't be able to distinguish one pie wedge from the next. If it is a diagram, they won't be able to distinguish where one shape ends and the next begins. Many presenters have a template mandated by the organization, so the core colors are already set for them. But when you are creating a visual, you will be selecting the colors yourself.

How can you be certain that the colors you choose will have enough contrast? Most presenters, like myself, don't have a design background and can't just look at two colors and know if they have enough contrast. It isn't enough to look at the colors on your computer screen. Laptop and flat-screen monitors are far brighter than projectors and give you a distorted perception of how much contrast exists between two colors. Instead, make sure the colors have enough contrast by using the international standard tests for color contrast.

A number of years ago, the World Wide Web Consortium (W3C) created a standard that tests the contrast between two colors. They developed it to help Web developers create easily readable websites. You can use these two tests to make your slides readable. Both tests are calculations that use the Red, Green and Blue (RGB) attributes of the two colors to determine if there is enough difference between them.

I've made this easy for presenters by creating an online Color Contrast Calculator that allows you to test the difference between two colors you are considering for your slides. Just go to **www.ColorContrastCalculator.com** to use this tool. You enter the red/green/blue values for each color and it tells you whether the colors pass the two tests. The results indicate not only whether the colors passed the test or not, but what the score was in relation to the minimum contrast score as indicated by the test parameters. If you are very close to passing the test, you can make the decision of whether to use the colors or not. The page also contains detailed instructions on how to find the RGB attributes of a color in PowerPoint and some ideas on what you can do to improve the contrast of two colors if they don't pass the tests. You can also use this tool as an objective viewpoint when discussing color choice with colleagues.

Choose Fonts that are Big Enough for the Room and Screen Size

The second aspect of slide design is the selection of font for the text on the slide. The first decision is to select the font to use on your slides. Research suggests that sans-serif fonts, like

Arial, Calibri, or Verdana, are easier to read when projected. In my workshops, I display a slide that has two sentences shown in four fonts: a script font, Times New Roman, Arial, and Calibri. I then ask the audience which text is easiest to read. Every time the audience clearly indicates that the sentences in Arial and Calibri are much easier to read. I don't need to share the details of the academic research that shows why the sans-serif fonts are easier to read, the audience comes to that conclusion on their own.

There are a number of different sans-serif fonts that you can choose from. Some presentation designers suggest that you avoid the built-in PowerPoint fonts and select a downloaded font that will be unique. I disagree with this advice for typical corporate presentations. Many of your presentations will end up being sent to others who will view them on a computer that doesn't have that downloaded font. When PowerPoint encounters a font it does not have, it selects a substitute font that could make the text unreadable or make it move all over the screen because of different spacing in different fonts. For this reason I suggest you stick to the standard sans-serif fonts like Arial, Calibri, or Verdana. Calibri is now the default font in PowerPoint and it has one advantage over other sans-serif fonts. Since Calibri has monospaced numbers, you can use the decimal tab feature in PowerPoint to align the numbers in a column and every number in the column will also be aligned. If you are reporting financial information, you will find this combination makes your life much easier.

The second decision is to select text that is big enough to be easily read by your audience. When I am asked in my workshops, "How big a font should I use on my slides?" the only truly correct answer is, "it depends."

I've heard a variety of answers to this question from different commentators. Some quote a particular point size and some use ratios depending on certain parameters. I am sure you would agree that the text should be larger than the record I have seen for the smallest font used on a slide – four point! I had to enlarge the slide just to see it was text instead of a thick line.

To properly answer the font size question, I did the research to come up with a way I could determine an appropriate font size that is easy to read. I started by considering visual acuity. This is the term used for how well we see. It is what the optometrist measures using the eye chart that starts with the large "E" at the top and the letters gradually get smaller in the lines below. They determine your visual acuity based on how tall a letter you can clearly see at what distance. It is important that we have the letters on our slides large enough so most people can see them.

The next challenge was to figure out what level of visual acuity I should assume for most audiences. To answer the average vision question, I turned to the standard used for road signs in North America. There is a manual for designers of road signs that specifies how big the letters should be in order for the text to be read at a certain distance from the sign. So I used these standards and the visual acuity measurement standards to determine that road signs assume approximately 20/35 vision (20/20 is perfect vision). So, to be conservative, I assumed 20/40 vision. It is one of the standard measurements and means that someone with 20/40 vision needs to stand 20 feet away from an object to see clearly what someone with perfect vision can see standing 40 feet away from the object.

I then used a projector to calculate the ratio of the height of a standard Arial font to the width of the projected image. This allows me to know how tall a letter of a particular point size will be on a screen of a certain size.

Using the assumptions of 20/40 vision and that the image fills the screen, I calculated the maximum distance that an audience member should be from the screen to comfortably read a font of a certain size. Now I can answer the font size question based on research, not on a feeling. There is no one single answer; it depends on screen size and the distance of the furthest person in the room.

What I have done is put all of this work into two easy-to-use tables that are available for you to download for free from my website. One table is for common projector and screen setups that use the 4:3 screen size ratio. The second table is for widescreen setups that are used by some newer projectors and flat screen TVs being used as presentation displays. Go to **www.PPtFontSizeTable.com** and you will see the links to download the tables in Adobe PDF format. You are free to tell others about the link and encourage them to use it to make sure that their audiences will be able to read the text on their slides.

In my workshops I show a slide that has text in different point sizes to demonstrate how easy or hard it is to read large or small text. I ask the audience to tell me what point sizes are easy to read. Inevitably they see how hard it is to read small text on the slide. They agree with the advice I give when I am asked for a quick answer that will work most of the time. I suggest 36-44 point fonts for slide headlines (titles) and 24-32 point for main slide text. I'll sometimes use 18 or 20 point text for graph labels or callout text, but this is about the smallest text that works in most of the rooms used for business presentations.

Avoid Distracting Elements

When you have images or other graphics as part of the slide background, it causes the audience to focus on the background instead of your content. Anything that takes the focus away from your message can contribute to confusing the audience. Consider why you are using a background graphic. If it is because you feel that you want your slides to be more visual, use the methods described in Chapters 12 to 21 to create effective visuals instead of using a background graphic. If it is because your template has a white background that you want to spice up, change the background color to a slight gradient of a light color which will give a more pleasing background for your slides. A plain background allows the audience to focus on your message and the accompanying visuals instead of trying to figure out what the background image or graphic represents.

Use these guidelines to create slides that are easy to see and read.

CHAPTER ELEVEN

Create An Effective Headline For Your Slide

Unless you are using a full slide sized image, I think you should have a headline at the top of each slide. The headline is a summary of the key message you want the audience to take away from the slide or point you are making. A headline should contain what the point is and why it is important to the audience.

Typically I see titles at the top of slides. How are titles and headlines different? First, a title is short, usually two to four words, whereas a headline is longer, usually six to ten words. Next, a title only tells you the topic being discussed and the presenter hopes that the audience figures out what the key message is. A headline is a sentence that is a summary of the key point you want the audience to remember. You do the work of figuring out the key point for the audience by creating a headline. Finally, a title can't stand on its own, it does not have meaning by itself. A headline stands on its own because it contains an entire thought.

The best source for learning about headlines is a newspaper, whether it is printed or online. If you look at newspapers, they use headlines that summarize the story. That way, the readers can get the point of the story and decide whether they want to read further details in the body of the story. For example, instead of a title, such as "Land Dispute," a news organization will write a headline, such as "Department officials urge resolution to riverfront land use dispute." See how much more compelling the headline is than the title?

Go to your favourite news site or grab your daily newspaper. Notice how the headlines are typically in the six to ten word range. On a popular news site I checked, the average headline of the top stories was eight-and-a-half words, with a range of six to twelve words for the headlines listed. I think you'll find a similar average and range on your news site or newspaper.

Using newspapers as a guide, you will see that headlines should be written in a more conversational tone instead of a formal tone. This makes them easy to understand and relate to. It draws the audience in to hear more from you and it is easier to write since you don't need to fuss over detailed grammatical rules. Be cautious of using too many acronyms or jargon words in the headline. Many organizations use the same acronym to mean more than one thing, and this can confuse the audience. If you must introduce an acronym, write out what it stands for in full the first time you use it in the presentation so it is clear what you are referring to with the acronym.

One good technique to use when trying to determine the headline of a slide is to ask yourself the question, "So what?" from the audience's point of view. Why would they care about the point you are making on this slide? Research tells us that people understand our message better when they know what our point means to them. Ask yourself the "So what?" question to hone in on the true meaning of this point to your audience. Here is an example of a headline being created on the topic of how many service reps you have at an office.

First attempt: We have 10 customer service reps.

Ask: So what?

Second attempt: We can process more orders.

Ask: So what?

Third attempt: We can serve more customers.

Ask: So what?

Fourth attempt: Customers wait less time to place their order.

Notice how each attempt got closer to the real reason that the number of customer service reps at this office matters to the audience. The audience cares about placing an order in the shortest possible time.

In some presentations I see the presenter use the same title on a number of slides, or they will use the same title on consecutive slides, adding "(continued)" to the end of the title. This is confusing to the audience because they can't figure out how all the points relate to each other across the multiple slides. Each slide should have its own headline, relevant to the point on that slide. Instead of repeating a title, start this section of your presentation with a slide summarizing the related points. Then, you can have one slide for each key point, with a headline that indicates why this point is important for the audience. It will be much easier for the audience to follow and understand.

In order to make headlines easy to read, leave space at the top of your slides for two lines of text in the font size you have chosen for the headline. This allows the words in the headline to avoid running into other elements on the slide.

Because a headline is a sentence, use sentence case instead of title case for the headline; it will be much easier to read. Headlines are best read when they are left aligned or center aligned. Right alignment of the headline is much harder for the audience to read, especially if it is two lines long. If your headline is not balanced because one or two words are on the second line, make it visually balanced by placing your cursor about half-way in the headline and break the line by pressing Shift+Enter. This allows the line to break with line spacing instead of paragraph spacing.

Examples of Headlines to Replace Titles

Starting each slide with a headline instead of a title is the single easiest thing you can do to improve the effectiveness of your slides. To make it easier for you to a create an effective headline, here are some examples of the slide title and the headline that replaced it. All of these examples come from slide makeovers I have done for client workshops or consulting assignments (some details may have been changed to protect the identity of the organization).

Title	Headline
RRSP/Pension Values	DB Pension gives more than double the retirement savings compared to RRSP
Alternative scenarios results	Most scenarios show significant loss vs. base scenario

Procurement Highlights-November 2011	Procurement results beat budget; Challenges include Thailand flood, 2012 Current View, Reseller Program
Spend and Cost Reduction Overview	Making progress on Cost Savings targets, need to pick up pace to meet targets by end of Fiscal Year
Key Challenges	Challenges include workmanship and increased demand for ABC model
Authority	Recognizing who has authority to bind the US Government
Leasing Activity	Total leasing activity showing strong overall absorption
Design	Design of prospective cohort study

Creating an effective headline is the easiest way to improve the effectiveness of your slides immediately. One way to test the effectiveness of your headlines is to look at only the headlines of your slides. Will the audience be able to understand the key points you are making only by looking at the headlines? This is a very stiff test and one that I won't pass every time. By setting the bar high, it makes us strive to write the best possible headlines so that the audience will understand our message clearly.

CHAPTER TWELVE

Selecting The Best Visual

A big challenge for many business presenters is how to create visuals for their slides instead of the text that tends to dominate most slides. Presenters think that they need some graphics or design training and expertise in order to conceive of and create presentation visuals. I think for most of the visuals needed in many business presentations, we can look to the lessons and experiences we had in grade school. Take a look at how some of the many learning experiences at school can result in simple and effective visuals for your presentations.

Grade school experience	Presentation visual
Stacking blocks on top of each other to see who could create the tallest stack	Column charts that show how measured values compare to each other
Playing with a model airplane and showing how it takes off and lands	Line charts that show trends up or down
Having the class line up from tallest to shortest	Bar charts showing ranked values
Discussing with a classmate about who gets the biggest piece of pizza	Show fractions of a whole using a pie chart

Watching a stream or river flow from one rock to another	Show movement through a process using a flow diagram
Understanding that your teacher had a boss above them, the principal	Show hierarchical relationships using an org chart diagram
Having a teacher show you a T-chart for comparing options	Use a table to compare options
Looking at the branches of a tree	Use a decision tree that shows different branches based on choices or options
Drawing a picture to go with a story you wrote	The power of using pictures to illustrate what we are saying
Telling time starts at twelve noon and proceeds clockwise	When showing any circular information, such as building the wedges of a pie chart or the steps of a continuous process diagram, start at the twelve noon position and build clockwise
Timelines in history books start on the left and proceed to the right	When showing sequential steps or concepts, start on the left and build each step moving left to right
Mathematical equations are first learned in a vertical orientation for addition and subtraction	When adding concepts to come to a conclusion, start at the top and add each concept to reach a conclusion at the bottom of the slide

| Learning how to understand a calendar | Use a calendar diagram to show when date specific events will happen |
| Learning how to use a map or globe to locate countries | Use a map to show geographic relationships in data |

Tapping in to the audience's base of knowledge and experience when creating visuals will enable your visuals to be instantly understood. As you see a greater variety of visuals, you will be able to create more visuals for your presentations. In Chapters 13 to 18, I will show you many presentation visuals and the best practices so you can create them yourself. By creating and using effective visuals, we can engage the audience to focus on the points we want them to remember instead of confusing them with overloaded text and data slides.

Another method of determining what visual to use is to look for words and phrases that suggest how the information is or could be organized, compared or related. Here is a table of words and phrases, and which visuals would best represent that information.

Word or phrase	Possible visual
Share of	Pie chart, grouped item comparison diagram
Trend	Line or column graph
Survey shows	Bar chart
Flow/Process	Process or flow diagram

Provinces/States/Countries	Map
Options/Choices	Decision tree diagram
Days/Months/Years	Gantt chart, Calendar diagram
Name of person/object	Photograph
On our website	Screen capture
Show an example	Video clip

This table is not meant to be an exhaustive list of words or phrases, nor is it meant to indicate every type of visual you should consider. It is meant to be a starting point to begin training your mind to think visually about some of the common words or phrases that are used in presentations.

Let's look at an example of how words can give us clues into the appropriate visual. If I have a slide that shows a comparison of the product returns in six local stores, the type of visual is not immediately clear. It depends on what the headline of the slide is. If the headline is, "Our store has lower returns than surrounding stores" it would suggest a column graph because we are comparing values. If the headline is, "Product returns higher in rural areas" then a map would be a good visual, because here we are looking at the geographical relationship of the data. In both cases, the words in the headline give us the clue as to what visual would be best. It is important to write the headline before you try to determine the visual.

Use Collections of Visuals to Get Ideas

I have no graphics or design background, so if I need some inspiration to get me thinking about what visual would fit a certain point, I look to some online resources. By seeing what visuals others have created, it can stimulate our own thinking of how our information can be presented. Here are some places I go to get ideas for visuals. Some of these sites offer visuals you can purchase and download, which might save you a lot of time. Even if you don't intend to buy a visual from the site, use them as an inspiration to create exactly what you need.

www.getmygraphic.com – This site, by graphic designer Michael Parkinson, contains graphics that are designed to be used in PowerPoint slides. You can purchase the visual you want, download it to your computer, and edit it in PowerPoint. There is a broad range of graphics, from simple to high-end professional graphic images.

office.microsoft.com – Part of the Microsoft Office online site contains templates that can be a good source of ideas for your own slides. Look for the templates that demonstrate content and show sample slide effects. These templates will show you how professional designers have conceptualized content and can spur your creativity to come up with ways to illustrate your points.

www.smartdraw.com – This software allows you to create numerous diagrams that can be useful visuals in a presentation. Even if you have no intention of purchasing the software, the examples of the types of visuals that they can create is a good source of ideas for creating visuals in PowerPoint.

www.diagrammer.com – This site, by top presentation design firm Duarte Design, allows you to select the type of diagram you want, purchase it, and download it for use on your slide. What I like about this site is the way it is organized. It very nicely walks you through steps to select the exact diagram to fit what you want to show.

www.charteo.com – This site has over 10,000 visuals you can purchase for use in PowerPoint. I like the breadth of visuals available, how they are organized, and the option to shade them in different colors to match your organization's template or colors.

www.visual-literacy.org/periodic_table/periodic_table.html – This website is a project from a group of academics who are studying ways to represent concepts visually. This page contains a large number of potential visual ideas organized into categories based on the periodic table of elements (there's the academic influence showing through). Notice that they have organized the visual methods (as they term them) by color to represent what you are trying to visualize (data, concept, strategy, etc.). They have added text colors and symbols to further categorize the methods on the basis of process vs. structure, detail vs. overview, and divergent vs. convergent thinking. It may seem a little too academic, but roll your mouse over any of the boxes in the table, and you will see a popup example of the visual relating to that method. It is interesting to see some of the examples, and it will give you ideas for your own visuals.

www.powerframeworks.com – A subscription site that has a large library of already created slides using visuals to represent concepts. You subscribe to the site and can then download any of the ready-to-use frameworks, as they call them. This is a good site for ideas and ready-made graphics for your presentations.

www.SlideMakeoverVideos.com – I have posted over 70 slide makeovers online where you can see a "before" slide that is often crowded with text or not designed well, and the "after" slide, which uses the ideas in this book to create a persuasive visual. I also give lessons that presenters can learn from the makeover that you saw. Use these videos as learning tools and as a way to get ideas of how to transform slides you may have that are similar to the ones shown in the videos.

As you visit websites and watch other visual media, take note of visuals that you like. Create a file of ideas on your computer to use as inspiration and as a growing resource you can easily refer to when working on your presentations.

In addition to the websites listed above, you can also use the SmartArt feature of PowerPoint to come up with ideas. While it may be tempting to just use one of the built-in SmartArt diagrams on your slide, my experience is that these built-in diagrams have too many assumptions and restrictions. These limitations restrict you from creating the exact diagram you want and delivering it in a way that makes it easy for the audience to understand. My suggestion is to use the SmartArt diagrams as another source for ideas, and create the diagram using the PowerPoint drawing tools.

CHAPTER THIRTEEN

Text Slides

While text on slides has gained a bad reputation amongst many presentation designers, I think text slides are still a good choice in many situations. In this chapter, we will look at bullet point slides, quotations, and textual information slides.

Bullet Points

A bullet point slide should not contain an overwhelming number of points. Here is an example of bullet points used effectively.

Critical Success Factors this year

- Control input costs
- Establish new markets for products
- Raise productivity by 1%
- Push R&D efforts:
    - User interface
    - Functionality

Best practices for bullet points:

- Bullet points are a way to visually show hierarchical information. The bullet points should break down the larger idea summarized in the slide headline. If the points you want to make are not hierarchical, then use text in shapes or just text on the slide instead of bullet points.

- Use bullet points instead of full sentences of text. A bullet point gives the audience the key idea or context you want them to have as you discuss this point. The bullet point should not be everything you intend to say. Your text slides should not be a transcript of your presentation.

- Use the six-by-six guideline to ensure that the text on your slide does not become your script. This guideline suggests that, on average, there should be no more than six words in a bullet point and there should be no more than six bullet points on a slide. This is not a hard rule, but it will help you distil your thoughts down to the key ideas you need the audience to remember.

- If you have written your bullet points using the above suggestions, there is no need for punctuation at the end of a bullet point, since it should not be a complete sentence. A bullet point is just a key thought, so it does not need punctuation at the end unless you want to include a question mark or exclamation point to add meaning to the phrase.

- Use filled bullet-point characters, such as a filled circle or filled square. These characters have enough presence on the slide to make it clear to the audience where each bullet point starts.

- Use the Title and Content layout in PowerPoint to make sure that the bullet points start at the same place on each slide and have the same formatting. This consistency allows the audience to spend less effort figuring out your slides and more time focusing on your message.

Quotations

It is sometimes necessary or desirable to use a quotation to support your point or to quote from a reference document to illustrate the point. Here are examples of quotations on slides.

"For time and the world do not stand still. Change is the law of life. And those who look only to the past or the present are certain to miss the future."

John F. Kennedy

"The purpose of the Organization is to contribute to peace and security by promoting collaboration among the nations through education, science and culture in order to further universal respect for justice, for the rule of law and for the human rights and fundamental freedoms which are affirmed for the peoples of the world, without distinction of race, sex, language or religion, by the Charter of the United Nations."

UNESCO Charter
(emphasis added)

Best practices for quotations:

- Always include the entire quotation. If you replace some of the words with "...", the audience will wonder what has been removed and consider whether you are trying to manipulate the quotation to mean something the speaker or author did not intend.

- Include the source of the quotation, whether it is a person or a document. Audiences need to know the source in order to give the quotation credibility.

- Consider adding a picture of the person if you are quoting someone. This gives the audience an emotional connection with the quotation.

- Use the Blank layout in PowerPoint for slides with quotations. Quotations should not have bullet points unless the source document has them. Place a text box on the slide and type or copy the quote in that text box. This gives you the flexibility to change the font size or formatting as needed.

- Give the audience context before you show the quote. They need to know the background, such as when it was said, under what circumstances, where was it said, who said it, why this person is important, what happened just before it was said, or why the person said it. Giving context prepares the audience to interpret the quote in the right way.

- When you show the slide with the quote, pause, turn towards the screen and stay silent for the few seconds that it takes to read the quote. I usually read the quote to myself to approximate how long it will take someone to read the quote. Then, turn back to face the audience and start your interpretation. If it is a short quote, you may read it to the audience, but it is not always necessary. Always give the audience time to read the quote when it appears on the screen. They naturally want to read it, so allow them to do so without interrupting them with your speaking. The reason for turning to face the screen is that people will look where you look, so if you look at the screen, they will look there as well and read the quote. When you turn back to face the audience, they have finished reading the quote and are ready to hear your insight.

- If there are a few words that you consider to be the key part of the quote, highlight those words so they stand out for the audience. You can do this when the quote first appears, but it is usually more effective if you highlight the key words as you are explaining them. Create a highlighter effect on the slide that looks like a highlighter being used on a book by placing a colored rectangle behind the key words.

Textual information

Text that is not hierarchical or a quotation should be shown on a simple slide containing lines of text or using shapes that group related text. Here are examples of simple text slides.

Product features

New slim design

Longer battery life

Higher resolution screen

New functions:

    Micrometer gap measurement

    Readings in under 0.5 seconds

Growth in account balance due to net new investments and fund growth

Net New Investments

Money contributed to the account less money taken out of the account

Fund Growth

Increase in value of the funds held in the account

Best practices for textual information:

- If the text you want to show is not hierarchical, then do not use bullet points. Just put the text on the slide. You should separate the text with a blank line so that the audience can easily distinguish each line of text from adjacent lines.

- When placing non-bulleted text on the slide, consider creating a slide layout in your PowerPoint template that is formatted so that all of the slides of this type have the text starting in the same position and the lines of text are separated by the same spacing.

- Another way to separate text is to place each line of text in a shape. This adds visual variety to the presentation and works well if there are groupings of text elements that are related. Placing the related text in the same shape indicates to the audience that those lines of text are related in some way.

- Use the Title Only or Blank slide layouts in PowerPoint for text inside shapes. It allows you the maximum area for the shapes, enabling you to make the shapes as large as possible so that the font is large enough to reasonably see.

- Choose colors for the shape fill and font that have high contrast, so the audience will easily be able to read what is inside the shape. Also make sure you set the text box formatting for each shape so that the text is large enough and it wraps properly inside the shape.

CHAPTER FOURTEEN

Graphs

Graphs (sometimes called charts) are a good way to visually show numeric information instead of pasting a spreadsheet on a slide. There are four types of graphs that are the most common: column, line, bar, and pie. While each type of graph does have some specific best practices, many of the best practices apply to all graphs. Here are examples of these four graph types and a variation of the column graph called a waterfall graph.

Column graph: shows differences in measured values and works best when there are six or fewer data points

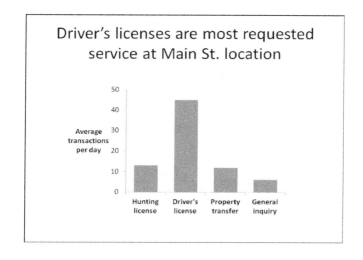

Line graph: shows differences in value over time and works well for many data points

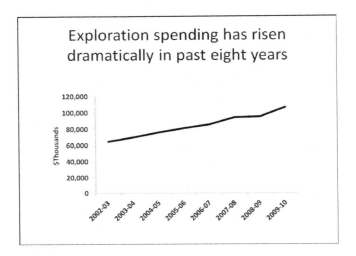

Bar graph: shows ranked values and works well for survey results

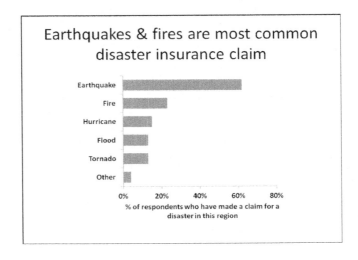

Pie graph: compares individual values to a whole

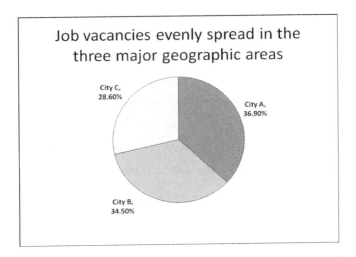

Waterfall graph: illustrates the components of the difference between a starting and ending value. A waterfall graph is a stacked column graph with one column set to no fill and no outline (making some columns seem to float above the axis).

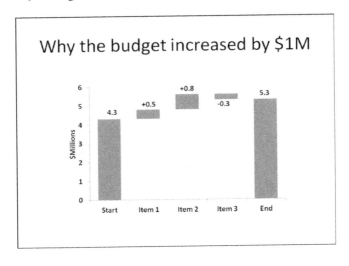

Best practices for graphs:

- It is preferable to create graphs in PowerPoint instead of creating them in Excel and copying the graph on to a slide. Graphs in PowerPoint are easier to edit and the colors will match the template. Do the calculations in Excel, then copy the required data into the PowerPoint graph data area to create the graph in PowerPoint.

- Select a 2-D version of the graph instead of a 3-D version because the third dimension makes it harder for the audience to understand the meaning of the graph.

- Arrange the data in a meaningful way instead of simply how it may have been calculated:

  - For column graphs, arrange the columns in order by smallest to largest, by time sequence, by geographic sequence, or by another sequence that fits with the point being made.

  - For bar graphs, you will typically arrange the bars from longest at the top to shortest at the bottom so the ranking of values is easy to see.

  - For pie graphs, arrange the pie wedges starting at the 12-noon position by most important to least important or by largest to smallest.

- Make sure that each graph has a headline that summarizes the point you are making. This helps the audience instantly understand the meaning of the graph. See Chapter 11 for tips on writing an effective headline.

- Remove any chart titles, as they are duplicative and take up space that can be better used to show the graph.

- Replace the legend with explanatory text that is closer to the data in the graph, such as data labels, text boxes, and axis titles. To add explanatory text that is not included in one of the PowerPoint features, add a text box outside the graph, enter the text, then move the text box on top of the graph where you want it to be.

- Remove the axis gridlines that are added by default. These extra lines distract the audience from the data in the graph.

- Clear the plot area so that the graph blends nicely into the slide.

- Reduce the amount of text on the measurement axis (the vertical axis on column or line graphs and the horizontal axis on bar graphs) so that the axis does not draw attention away from the data. Extra text can be removed by setting the unit parameter so that fewer values appear on the scale.

- In column or bar graphs, make the columns/bars wider so that they stand out better. To do this in PowerPoint, you need to reduce the space between the columns/bars (referred to as Gap Width in PowerPoint).

- To emphasize one column/bar/pie wedge, set the fill to a more visible color and set all other columns/bars/pie wedges to a muted color or to only have an outline. This way, the emphasized data stands out better.

- For line graphs, set the line thickness to at least four points so that it will be easy to see.

- If you want a cleaner-looking graph, consider removing the measurement axis and using data value labels instead. This works well for column or bar graphs where you have few data points and the data values will communicate the message easily.

- For column/bar/line graphs, don't start the measurement axis at a value that exaggerates the differences between the values. Once the audience sees that you are trying to fool them with the axis, your credibility will be diminished.

- If you want to compare the measured values to a standard or other reference value, add a dashed line on top of a column or line graph so the audience can easily see how the values in the graph measure against the reference value.

- If you want to add even more visual meaning to a graph, consider whether filling one or more portions of the graph with an image or photo would make the graph easier for the audience to understand your message. For example, in a column graph showing growth rates of two countries, you could fill each column with an image of the flag of that country, making the comparison more meaningful.

CHAPTER FIFTEEN

Diagrams

Diagrams are useful for showing non-numeric information or ideas. In this chapter, we will show examples and best practices for diagrams that show processes or flows, relationships, time-based information, and dashboard views of a situation.

Process or Flow Diagrams

Instead of a numbered list of steps in a process or flow of information/goods, use a process or flow diagram to illustrate how the steps relate to each other. Here are three examples of process or flow diagrams.

Box and arrow linear flow diagram: used for linear processes when you want the audience to easily distinguish between the work being done in each step, and activity or movement between the steps.

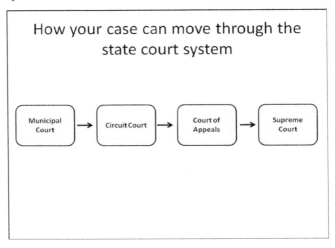

Chevron linear flow diagram: used for linear processes when each step is of equal importance and no distinction between types of activity is required.

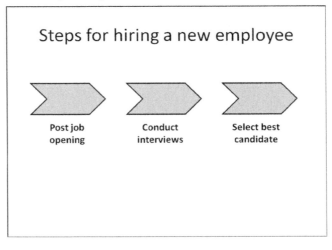

Continuous process diagram: used for processes that start again once a cycle is complete.

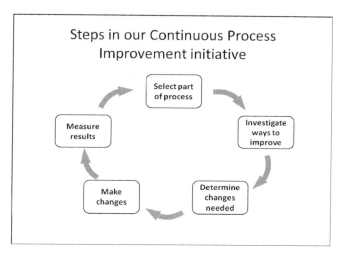

Best practices for process or flow diagrams:

- With the drawing tools in PowerPoint, use the shapes available to create the diagram. This is a better choice than using the SmartArt diagrams that are provided in the software or creating the diagram in a graphics program. You will have more flexibility in editing and building with animation when you create the diagram yourself using shapes.

- Include text descriptions for each step instead of numbers, symbols or colors. This makes each step clearer for your audience.

- You can use elements, such as graphic arrows or even photos of each step in the process, to increase the visual appeal of the diagram.

- If you have a complex or long process to illustrate, group related sections together so that the diagram has a maximum of six steps in it. You can create other slides to explain each step in more detail, if needed. See Chapter 21 for two techniques that can help explain complex processes.

- Use a text box to create a description that can be placed anywhere on the slide instead of restricting the text to inside a shape, such as a chevron, rectangle, triangle, or other shape.

Relationship Diagrams

Instead of trying to describe relationships between entities or concepts using paragraphs of text, it is better to illustrate the relationship using a diagram. Here are some examples of relationship diagrams.

Decision tree diagram: used to illustrate the relationship between questions and possible outcomes during decision making.

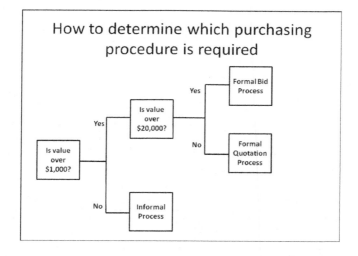

Organizational chart diagram: used to illustrate hierarchical relationships. This can be between staff in an organization or between items that have a hierarchical relationship.

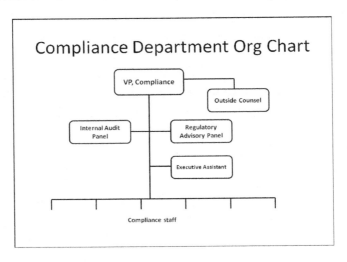

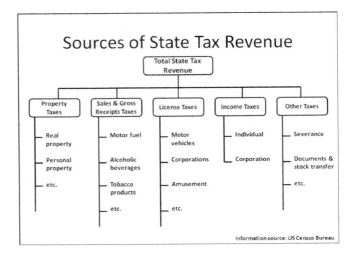

Venn diagram: used to illustrate an overlapping relationship.

Causal relationship diagram: used to show the relationship between a cause and the resulting effects.

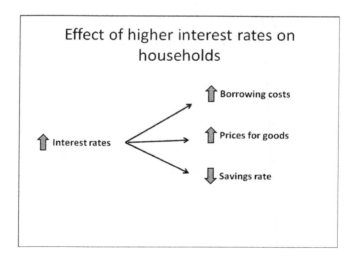

Equation diagram: used to illustrate the relationship between reasons or arguments and the conclusion to be reached.

Approving water & sewer infrastructure projects benefits residents

Create jobs and economic development

\+   Stewardship of the environment

\+   Improve health & safety for residents

―――――――――――――――――――――――――

Increase in quality of life for residents

Best practices for creating relationship diagrams:

- With the drawing tools in PowerPoint, use the shapes available to create the diagram. This is a better choice than using the SmartArt diagrams that are provided in the software or creating the diagram in a graphics program. You will have more flexibility in editing and building with animation when you create the diagram yourself using shapes.

- To draw a perfect square or circle in your diagram, hold down the Shift key while drawing the shape.

- To draw a horizontal or vertical line in your diagram, hold down the Shift key while drawing the line (it restricts the line to 45 degree increments from horizontal or vertical, so you can be slightly off with your drawing and the line will still be perfect).

- To move objects a small amount on the slide, for example, when you are trying to line up two objects, use the arrow keys to move the object a small distance. Holding the Ctrl key down while using the arrow keys gives the finest control as it moves the object one pixel at a time.

- Make a line or the outline of a shape at least 2.25 points thick, so it will be easy to see when viewed by the audience.

- Use fonts at least 18 point or larger, so the audience can read the labels on the diagram easily.

- Sometimes to get text exactly where you want it inside a shape, you should create the text box outside the shape and then drag it on top of the shape. This allows you more formatting flexibility than using the text option built into the shape.

- Each shape on a slide is on its own layer. These layers can be moved forward or backward as needed to create the exact diagram you need. Use the Bring Forward, Send Backward, Bring to Front, and Send to Back functions to move objects in front of or behind other objects on the slide.

Time-based Diagrams

When presenting information that is organized by time or date, it is common to simply list the information in chronological order. While this is accurate, it does not help the audience understand the information easily because we have been taught that time-based information is organized according to the clock and calendar. Here are two ways that time-based information can be illustrated for your audience.

Gantt chart: used to show scheduling of items along a timeline. The length of each bar denotes how long the event takes and the positioning of the bars shows when the event starts and finishes.

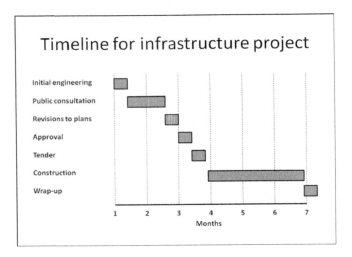

A timeline is also useful for showing when events occurred during the time span shown. A simple timeline is similar to a Gantt chart except the shapes indicating the events are all the same size and do not denote a length of time. Where the shape is located along the timeline indicates when the event occurred.

Calendar diagram: used to show when events occur based on the calendar.

Important dates for Real Property
Taxes in Marin County

July	August	Sept
1		

July 1: County assessor completes roll

Oct	Nov	Dec
	1	10

Nov 1: First installment notice sent

Dec 10: First installment due

Jan	Feb	March
	1	

Feb 1: Second installment notice sent

April	May	June
10		

April 10: Second installment due

Source of information: County of Marin

Best practices for creating time-based diagrams:

- Instead of using a graphics program to create your time-based diagram, use the drawing tools in PowerPoint. By using lines, shapes, text boxes, or tables, you can create the diagrams that you need. Three functions in PowerPoint are very helpful when creating Gantt charts (and any other diagrams as well). The first is the Distribute function, which allows you to evenly distribute objects within a certain area. For example, this is how you create a perfectly spaced timeline of months in a Gantt chart. The second is the Align function, which allows you to line up shapes, such as text and a rectangle so that the middle of the text is lined up with the middle of the rectangle. And the third, the Group function allows you to group a text box and a rectangle so that they can be moved together and stay aligned. Using these functions will allow you to quickly create a Gantt chart in PowerPoint.

- If you need to use a diagram created in another software program, such as a project management software package, use the export function of the software to create an image that you can paste into your slide. This approach may give you greater accuracy, but you will now have less flexibility because the information is not changeable in image format (since it is now like a photo).

- Make sure you identify the time scale in the diagram. In a Gantt chart, include a marked timeline along the top or bottom so the audience knows what the length of each bar means as shown in the Gantt chart example earlier. In a calendar diagram, label the days, weeks or months so the audience can understand the diagram easily.

- It is often a good idea to indicate the separations between the time periods which will aid in understanding of the diagram. On a Gantt chart, add vertical lines that indicate the time periods (usually weeks or months), and on calendar diagrams add lines that separate the days/weeks/months (these lines are automatically added if you use a table to create the calendar diagram).

- Make sure you have added labels that identify each item on the diagram. On a Gantt chart, make sure each bar has a label on the left side or as part of the bar itself. On a calendar diagram, make sure the specific events are labelled, and you indicate where on the calendar that event is located.

- You may have to place a shape on a calendar diagram to indicate when an event takes place that covers up part of the underlying calendar. If this happens, make the fill color of the shape semi-transparent so that the audience can still somewhat see the calendar, and they will still know how this event fits in to the overall diagram.

- Create your calendar diagram based on the span of dates that you need to show. If all of the dates are within one month, use a monthly calendar that shows all the days of the month, as on a wall or desk calendar. If the dates span over two or three months, you still may be able to use monthly calendars beside each other on the slide, as long as it does not get too crowded. When the dates span over three to 12 months, you can no longer use monthly calendars that show every day, because it is too busy on the slide. In these cases, use a yearly format that just shows the months and not the days within the months. Add text boxes with the specific dates to show when an event happens, as shown in the Calendar diagram example.

If you make your time-based diagram look like a calendar that your audience sees regularly, on their computer, on their smartphone, or printed, the diagram will make immediate sense to the audience and your point will be easy to understand.

Dashboard Diagrams

A dashboard slide gives the audience a quick snapshot of how the organization or area of interest is performing. Executives use them for quick visual updates on organizational performance and investors can use them for quick updates on how their investments are doing. Here are two examples of dashboard diagrams.

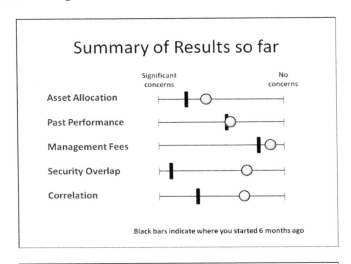

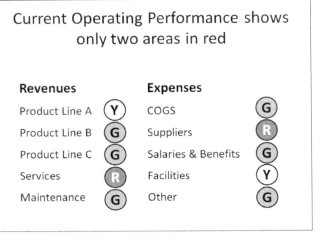

Best practices for using dashboard diagrams:

- The first step in creating an effective dashboard diagram is to decide on the correct metrics to use. This is done in conjunction with the people responsible for that area or external experts. When selecting the metrics, make sure that you will be reporting numbers that have context. A single number on its own does not have context since you can't tell if that number is acceptable or not. By comparing the current value to one in the past or a standard, the audience will have context. Since many dashboards use indicators of how acceptable or unacceptable the measured results are, get agreement on what constitutes an acceptable or unacceptable result, and any gradients in between. It is critical to get the definitions of each result or end of the spectrum correct before designing the diagram.

- Once the metrics are well defined, the next step is to decide how to show the metrics. If you decide to use a common approach of stoplight indicators, with red indicating an area that needs immediate attention, yellow an area of concern, and green indicating acceptable performance, remember that some people may not be able to interpret the colors green or red due to red-green color blindness. Medical research suggests that this condition affects approximately one in ten Caucasian males. If you use the stoplight approach, include the first letter of the color (R, Y, or G) in a contrasting text color so everyone is clear on what the indicator means. Don't restrict your indicators to just the stoplight colors. Use indicator arrows (↑ or ↓) to indicate trends. Use a checkmark or 'X' (☑ or ☒) to indicate acceptable or unacceptable situations. A thumbs up or thumbs down symbol (👍 or 👎) can also work. By using a variety of indicators, it makes it more visually interesting for the viewer.

- You can also decide to use a sliding scale to allow for finer gradients on the scale from acceptable performance to unacceptable performance. Make sure you define how to calculate where on the scale the measured value is and display it in a way that is easy to understand. Typically in the Western world we see the scale going from left to right with the lower scores or unacceptable performance on the left and better scores or acceptable performance on the right. A sliding scale allows you to place an indicator on the scale showing where the metric was previously and then showing where the performance is currently. This can be helpful for the audience as it allows them to see how much progress has been made in those areas that need improvement.

- Don't get trapped into thinking that every metric must be reduced to a single indicator or value. Some metrics are more complex and may need more information to allow an audience to properly interpret the results. You may need to show a trend using a line graph along with the goal that is trying to be achieved. In this way, the audience can see that performance is better than last year, is improving each month, but that the goal has not yet been achieved. This is a better interpretation than a simple red circle showing that the goal has not been achieved this year.

- Consider how the audience will want to see the detailed information behind the dashboard slide. Often you will start with a broad overview in a dashboard slide, and then go deeper into each area with additional graphs or diagrams so they can interpret the broad indicators properly. There are many ways to break down the overall results. You could dive deep by geographic area if that makes sense, or by product or service grouping if that will be more helpful. Sometimes the audience will want to break down the information by first looking at what metrics need attention, regardless of what area they come from. Use your audience analysis to determine how they want to see it broken down and perhaps give some options with a non-linear approach to building and delivering the presentation.

CHAPTER SIXTEEN

Comparisons

When you want to show the comparison of two or more items, you have a number of choices on how to visually show the comparison. In this chapter, we will discuss comparison tables, points in time comparisons, proportional shape comparison diagrams, and grouped items comparison diagrams.

Comparison Tables

A comparison table makes it easy for the audience to compare how different items or options measure on the selected criteria. A comparison table is better than putting each item or option on its own slide because it allows the audience to have context for the comparison.

Both options for CR62 are viable

Criteria	Option 1	Option 2
Farmland impact	3 new ditch crossings required	Utilize existing right-of-way corridor
Relocations	None	3 residential
Impact on Village	Minimizes future impacts	Results in additional traffic flow in village
Construction costs	Higher	Lower

Best practices for comparison tables:

- In the table, the general layout is to have the criteria in the first column, and each subsequent column shows how each option/item measures against the criteria.

- You can use the Table feature in PowerPoint to add a table easily to your slide. Select a design that is simple and clean, not having distracting colours and shading that will take attention away from your information. You can use tabs within a cell to help line up numbers or text.

- You can also use a text box to create a table. Add tabs to the ruler to set where the columns of information start. You can use a decimal tab to make numeric information line up easily (if each individual number needs to be aligned, use a font like Calibri that has mono-spaced numbers). Add lines to make the separation between columns more distinct. To create lines that are perfectly vertical or horizontal, hold the Shift key down while drawing the line, since it will automatically correct for minor changes in the line direction.

- When describing how each item measures on the criteria in a comparison table, minimize the amount of text as much as possible so you do not have excessive text on the slide. Use the tips given in Chapter 6 to reduce the text to the essential message the audience needs to hear.

- Make the headings of the table stand out by putting them in a bold and/or larger font than the rest of the text. Consider aligning them in the center of each column so they stand out from the left aligned text or right aligned numbers.

- If you are copying a table of information from Excel, there are five options to consider for pasting the copied cells into PowerPoint. No single option is the best for each situation, so consider the advantages and disadvantages of these five options:

  - **Basic Paste (Ctrl+V):** *Advantages:* pastes the data as a PowerPoint table, saving time over copying and pasting each cell; *Disadvantages:* PowerPoint default colors and fonts not adopted by pasted text; text does not resize when you resize the table

  - **Paste Special – Excel Worksheet Object:** *Advantages:* object resizes text when it is resized; *Disadvantages:* PowerPoint default colors and fonts not adopted by pasted object; entire Excel worksheet is copied into PowerPoint file, leading to large file size and ability of anyone who has the file to see the entire Excel worksheet, including confidential data on other sheets

  - **Paste Special – Formatted Text:** *Advantages:* since the Excel cells are inserted as a text box with tabs to create the columns, the text box can be animated to appear one row at a time and text box formatting, such as adding or changing the types of tabs, is allowed; *Disadvantages:* PowerPoint default colors and fonts not adopted by pasted text; text does not resize when you resize the text box

- *Paste Special – Metafile Picture: Advantages:* text of image gets resized clearly (better than bitmap image option); keeps Excel formatting with transparent background; *Disadvantages:* no editing possible

- *Paste Link – Excel Worksheet Object: Advantages:* object on slide will update as Excel data is updated in source file because the slide and the Excel file are linked; object resizes text when it is resized; *Disadvantages:* Security warning appears whenever PowerPoint file is opened even though only notification is really to update data from source file; PowerPoint default colors and fonts not adopted by pasted object

- When using a table of numbers, instead of positive or negative signs to indicate the difference when comparing a measured value, consider using symbols such as up or down arrows (↑ or ↓), thumbs up or down (👍 or 👎), happy or sad faces (☺ or ☹), or checkmarks and X's (☑ or ☒). These universal indicators are more visual and will demonstrate to the audience whether the number is showing good performance or poor performance. A positive or negative difference does not tell the audience whether the number is good or not, which may lead to confusion if they can't figure it out.

Two points in time Comparison Diagrams

When you want to compare the same measured value at two points in time, you can use a comparison diagram that shows the previous and current measurements.

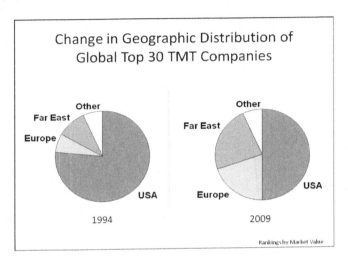

Best practices for creating two points in time comparison diagrams:

- For side-by-side comparison diagrams, make sure each graph or diagram is the same size and is illustrating the same measurement. You want this to be an "apples to apples" comparison. If the measurements are different or the graphs are a different size, the audience will not be able to trust the point you are making, since it will look like the comparison is incorrect.

- When using graphs in a side-by-side diagram, make sure you have used the best practices for graphs described in Chapter 14. With multiple graphs on the slide, any distracting elements make it even harder for the audience to focus on the message you are delivering.

Proportional shapes Comparison Diagrams

When you only have a few values to compare and want to dramatically show the differences between the values, consider a diagram that shows shapes that are proportional to the measured values. The difference in size shows the dramatic comparison to the audience.

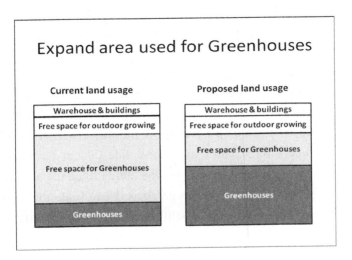

Best practices for creating proportional shape comparison diagrams:

- Select the same shape for each value you are comparing. The two most common shapes are rectangles and circles.

- The audience will compare the area of the shape, not the length of a side or the diameter of a circle. Remember the calculations for area from our grade school days: the area of a rectangle is *height x width* and the area of a circle is πr^2 where r is the radius of the circle. To draw a perfect square or perfect circle, hold the Shift key down before you start drawing with the rectangle or oval shape tool.

- You will need to convert the values into sizes of shapes that will fit on the slide. PowerPoint allows you to specify the exact size of a shape in standard measurement units such as inches or centimetres (cm). I have found it easiest to use centimetres because it is a base 10 measurement system and it makes the math easier. The largest shape that reasonably fits on a slide is 15 cm tall, so keep that in mind when scaling your values. For example, if I had values of 400 and 60 to represent using rectangles, I might consider making one side the same size and show the difference in the other dimension. I can't make one side 20 cm because that would be too big to fit on the slide. Since the shapes are being used to show proportions, I can scale the sizes so that the proportion is still the same. I might scale down the values by a factor of 5 so I can have shapes that are 80 cm^2 and 12 cm^2. My shapes could then have one side that is 6 cm and then I calculate what the other side would be, 13.33 cm and 2 cm in this example.

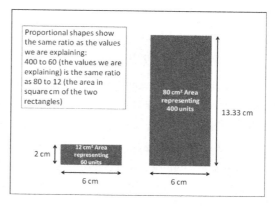

This allows me to have perfectly proportional shapes on the slide representing my two values.

- To set the exact dimensions of a shape in PowerPoint, you can enter the measurements of each side in the fields provided in the toolbar or in the formatting dialog box for the shape. I find it easiest to enter the measurement in cm by first entering the value, followed by the cm measurement unit label. Even if your system defaults to inches, this entry gives you the exact dimension you need and the system does the conversion to your local units of measurement. For a circle, you will need to set both the height and width, which is the desired diameter of the circle. Going back to grade school math, the diameter is two times the radius of the circle.

- To make it easier for those in the audience who relate to numbers, add text box labels either inside or outside the shape. The label should identify the item and state the value being represented, as you see in the example above.

- Due to space limitations on a slide, this approach usually works if you have four or fewer values to represent. More than four shapes can get confusing for the audience.

- If it will help the audience understand the message, you can fill each shape with a photo that adds meaning to what is being represented. For example, you may want to fill a shape with a photo of the object being represented, such as the vegetable being grown on that portion of land, or the flag of the country that the data represents.

Grouped items Comparison Diagrams

As an alternative to a graph, you can also use groups of the same shape to show the value of different items or aspects.

Results of 100 point Assessment Checklist

Excellent (7)   Acceptable (48)   Not acceptable (45)

Best practices for grouped items comparison diagrams:

- Always use the same shape for each grouping. If you change shapes, the audience may interpret the visual incorrectly because they will assign importance to the size or other aspects of the two shapes. You can use a simple shape, such as a circle or square, or you can use an icon or vector drawing such as an outline of a person if that will be more meaningful.

- Separate groups of related items to show the size of the measured value. Don't randomly position all of the shapes in one large group of different colored shapes. The audience won't be able to find and count all the shapes of each color to calculate the values you are representing.

- Use a heading for each grouping to make it clear what the group represents. Include the value if you feel some audience members will want to see it numerically as well.

- You can use color to add additional meaning to the shapes. You can use a Red, Yellow, Green color scheme as would be used in the example above to indicate Not Acceptable (Red), Acceptable (Yellow), and Excellent (Green). If there is a binary interpretation, such as stop/go or yes/no, you can just use Red and Green. Select colors that will be meaningful to the audience and aid in their understanding of the visual.

CHAPTER SEVENTEEN

Multimedia

Multimedia used to be hard to incorporate in a presentation, but the tools available today make it much easier. Audiences expect you to be using photos, audio clips, and video clips, the topics we will discuss in this chapter.

Photos

Photographs are used to show your point instead of text that can only describe with words what you want the audience to understand about a person, place, object, emotion, or activity.

Best practices for using photographs:

- One source for photos is the Microsoft media library. You can search this library through the Clip Art function of PowerPoint if you are connected to the Internet. Select that you only want to search photos, not Clip Art or other media, and ensure that it is set to search the online or Web collections. In the Microsoft media library search, it is usually best to search using either one word, or two words separated by a plus sign (+) instead of a long string of words. A better selection of results is generated using these search techniques. You can insert a photo directly from the search results without any payment required for the usage.

- Another source of photos is from the stock photography websites that collect professional photographs and make them available for purchase. Two examples of these types of sites are **istockphoto.com** and **shutterstock.com**. These sites contain millions of photos that have been screened by editors before being allowed on the site. They allow you to search for a photo that matches what you are looking for. Depending on the site, you may have to exclude other media, such as audio or video, from your search. These search functions work more like a Web search, so use multiple words in your search term to return a specific set of photos that match your desired criteria. Once you have found a suitable photo, purchase the appropriate resolution (usually 1024 x 768 if you plan to use the photo full-slide, 800 x 600 for most other uses) and download it to your computer. Now you can insert the saved photo on your slide.

- A third source of photos is the media library of Wikipedia, called Wikimedia Commons, at **commons.wikimedia.org**. This image sharing database of millions of images is made available for presenters to use, subject to the license specified by the image owner. Each image states how the owner has opted to make it available. This collection is particularly strong in photos of historical figures and map images. Make sure you follow the usage guidelines when using images from this site.

- A fourth source of photos is photo-sharing websites, such as **Flikr.com**. These sites allow anyone to upload their photos and share them with the world. You can search for a photo that matches your point among all the photos that have been uploaded. Your search results depend on how well the photographer tagged the photo after they uploaded it, as the sites rely on users to tell you what the photo is about. Due to many of the photos not being released for use in presentations or for commercial purposes, make sure you restrict your search to only those photos that are allowed to be used, and follow all license terms stated on the site.

- A fifth source of photos is from various government departments that are made available for use without charge. Since the photos have been taken on behalf of the citizens of the country, many of the photos are made available for use, often only requiring a short statement of the source of the photo on your slide. The availability varies from country to country, so check with your local sources to see if they have photos that you could use.

Some departments or agencies in the U.S. that have photo libraries available include the Bureau of Land Management, U.S. Department of the Interior, U.S. Geological Survey, and The National Oceanic and Atmospheric Administration. They have a wide variety of photos, from scenery to people engaged in activities to animals and weather events.

• A final source is from photos that you have taken. Your own photos can give you exactly the photo you need. Follow good photography practices, such as having enough lighting and using the best camera settings to ensure you get a clear photo. If you are taking the photo on behalf of your employer, make sure you understand who owns the rights to the photo and how it can be used.

• Regardless of where you source the photo, you may need to reduce the resolution of the photo when using it in PowerPoint. A high-resolution photo will make your PowerPoint file grow very large, too large in many cases to be e-mailed to others. Before you insert the photo on a slide, reduce the resolution using a program such as the Microsoft Office Picture Manager (usually found in the Microsoft Office Tools folder). If the photo is already in PowerPoint, use the Compress Pictures function to eliminate the extra pixels in high-resolution photos that PowerPoint will never use for your presentation. The quality of the photo is not changed, but the size of the PowerPoint file can be reduced dramatically.

• Even though there are many photos on the Internet, in most cases, you can't use them in your presentation without permission from the owner of the photo. All photos are copyrighted by the owner automatically, and publishing the photo on the Web does not change the protection given to the photo by the copyright law. Before using any photo, make sure you have permission from the owner (which may not be the photographer in some cases) and you have read the license that specifies how the photo may be used.

- When you need to give credit on your slide in order to use the photo, do so in small text in a lower corner of the slide, and using a text color that is more muted than the regular text on the slide. This way, the source is credited, but the text does not take away from the message on the slide.

- Once you have inserted the photo on your slide, PowerPoint gives you tools that you can use to modify the photo to suit your needs. You can use the crop tool to cut away part of the photo. This will help the audience focus on the important part of the photo and not be distracted by other elements in the photo. You can adjust the brightness and contrast of the photo or change the coloring of it to achieve a different effect that captures the attention of the audience. PowerPoint also gives you a tool that will make one color transparent, which can help in removing the background in some photos and making the subject of the photo stand out. You don't need fancy photo-editing software to achieve some interesting looks for your photos.

- You can make the photo look even more interesting by changing the borders of the photo. Instead of the regular rectangular border, you can use the photo as the fill color for a shape, and have it with a circular, oval, or rounded rectangular border. Experiment with these techniques to see if they could add interest, without losing the impact of your photo.

- When you use a photo in your presentation, make sure you introduce it first, before you show it on the screen. Without the appropriate context, your audience may come to the wrong conclusion about the photo before you have a chance to explain it. You can use the animation features of PowerPoint that I will explain in Chapter 20 to sequence the display of the photo on the slide.

Audio Clips

Audio clips are used to allow the audience to hear someone's voice (including tone and inflection) instead of just reading their words on the screen.

Best practices for using audio clips:

- When using an audio clip, place a picture of the person who is speaking on the slide so the audience has a visual image to go along with the words they are hearing.

- Audio clips should be no longer than 60 seconds, and preferably closer to 30 seconds long. Longer clips will start to bore the audience. Edit your audio clip down so that only the relevant pieces of the recording are played.

- The MP3 format is the best audio format since it is very common and PowerPoint plays it easily.

- Make sure that you have a high-quality audio clip, with no distortion or background noise. When the clip is amplified during the presentation, these noises will be much more prominent and will distract the audience from the message you want them to hear. If you can't get rid of other noises on the audio clip, consider putting the text of what is being said on the slide, so people can read it if they can't hear the words clearly.

- Adjust the volume of the audio clip or the volume of your computer so that it will be easy for the audience to hear the audio during the presentation.

- Use the function in PowerPoint to include audio on your slide instead of playing it from a media player. This allows you to use the controls in PowerPoint to play the clip when you want to and adjust the volume within the presentation.

- Similar to using photos, introduce an audio clip properly before you play it for the audience. Give them the context, and explain who they are listening to and what you want them to pay attention to in the clip. With the correct context, the audience will be prepared to listen to the audio and understand how it reinforces the point you are making.

Video Clips

Video clips are used to show the audience what you are talking about instead of you just describing the scenario.

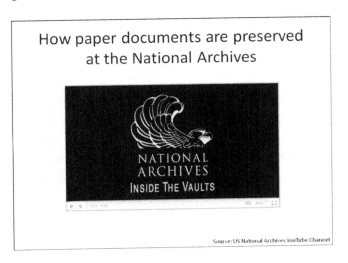

Source: US National Archives YouTube Channel

Best practices for using video clips:

- Do not use video clips, especially online videos, just because you think they are "cool." A video clip should only be used when it illustrates your point better than the other visual choices you considered.

- An effective video clip makes only one point and should be no more than 60 seconds long (preferably closer to 30 seconds). If the video clip tries to make more than one point, the audience will not be able to figure out which point they should pay attention to. For example, you could have a video clip of a plant manager speaking about the improvement they experienced due to implementing a certain policy. You would not want to use the entire interview where they spoke about production levels, a recent retirement celebration in the cafeteria, or renovations to the plant, because your point about the improvement due to the policy would be lost amongst the other information.

- Use video-editing software when you need to edit a longer video clip into a shorter clip that makes just one point. Some free video editing options include the Movie Maker package that Microsoft makes available for download, iMovie on a Mac, or some online video-editing sites. You can use one of these options to do the editing yourself instead of hiring a video-production company. Always save the edited video to a new file name so that you do not overwrite the original video file.

- While we can't give you legal advice in this book and you should always check with a qualified attorney on any legal matters, we can advise that you will need permission from the owner of the video, and anyone in the video, in order to use it in your presentation. You should have signed video release forms from everyone in the video if you have shot the video yourself. If the video was created by someone else, make sure you have their permission to use it in your presentation. This applies for motion pictures, online videos, and those you purchase. If you have shot and created the video yourself, check your employment contract to see if you own the video or your employer does.

- In the Windows version of PowerPoint, the preferred video file format is the Windows Media Video (WMV) format. There are other common formats that will work in all versions of PowerPoint, such as AVI and MPEG formats. Newer versions of PowerPoint, starting with PowerPoint 2007, allow QuickTime MOV files to be inserted on a slide. If you receive or create a video that is not in one of the common video file formats, you can convert the file using an online-conversion site or use video-conversion software on your computer to convert the file to the WMV format. If you capture a video on a mobile device, such as a smartphone, it may need to be converted, since there is no consistent standard video format for mobile devices.

- When preparing a video clip for use in a presentation, you want the frame size and frame rate to be set to give the best viewing experience for the audience. The frame size should be large enough so that the video is crisp and clear when shown. Usually a minimum frame size of 640 x 480 should be used. With live action video, try to use a frame rate of 30 frames per second (fps), since that is what the audience is used to seeing when watching TV or a movie.

- The preferred method for including a video clip on a slide is to use the PowerPoint function for inserting a video file. This allows you to control the playing of the video using the regular PowerPoint video and animation controls. This will only work for those formats supported by your version of PowerPoint.

- For video files that are not natively supported by your version of PowerPoint, you can still include them in your presentation by linking to them from a slide. Take a screen capture of the video, and insert the image on a slide. Create a hyperlink from the image to the video file on your computer. When you activate the hyperlink, your computer will open the video in your default video player on top of your PowerPoint presentation. You can use the video player controls to start or stop the video, adjust the volume, and make the video larger on the screen. When you are finished playing the video, close the video player program, and you will return to the PowerPoint presentation. This method is not as smooth as inserting the video on a slide, but it may be the only way you can include certain video clips in your presentation.

• In PowerPoint 2007 and earlier versions, the video file is not embedded in the PowerPoint file, even though you have used the function to "Insert" the video file. If you are using one of these versions of PowerPoint and want to run the presentation on a different computer from the one that you created the presentation on, you will need to copy both the video file and the PowerPoint file to the other computer or a USB key you plan on using. To prevent the link breaking when the files are moved, make sure that the video file and PowerPoint file are in the same folder before the video file is inserted on the PowerPoint slide. This will create a relative link that should not be affected by moving the files to another computer.

• Similar to using photos or audio clips, introduce a video clip properly before you play it for the audience. In your introduction to the video, explain what the audience will see and what they should be looking for that illustrates your point. Explain why you are showing the clip, what it will be showing, and when during the clip they should pay the most attention to catch the important point. For example, if I am introducing a video testimonial, I might say, "I'd like you to hear from Denise Stewart, the office manager of the Main Street location. Listen about 15 seconds in as she describes the reduction in employee turnover they have experienced because of this training program. Let's watch this clip." Now your audience knows why they are watching the clip, and how it illustrates and reinforces a key point you are making.

- When the video clip is playing, you should face the screen because the audience will look where you are looking. When the clip is done, turn to face the audience again and continue with your presentation, explaining how the clip reinforces the point you are making.

CHAPTER EIGHTEEN

Incorporating Other Sources

There are other sources of information that you may want to include on your slides. In this chapter we will look at geographic information, screen captures, content from PDF documents, hyperlinks, and case studies.

Geographic Information

When the information you are presenting is geographically related, the best visual is usually a map, which can visually show the relationship like this example.

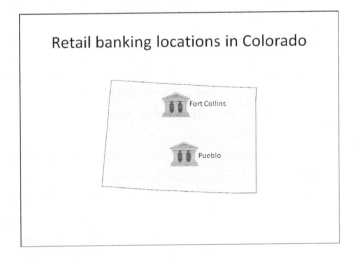

Best practices for creating maps:

- Make sure your map is accurate for the area being displayed. Select your map from a reputable source, which may include paying for a high-quality map of the area. If you want to use a screen capture of an online map site, make sure you read the usage guidelines for the site carefully and seek legal advice to ensure you can use the map. In Chapter 17 in the section on Photos, I mentioned the Wikimedia Commons site that contains many high quality maps you can use, subject to the usage restrictions of the owner.

- Sometimes your map will be a site drawing or building layout image. These images can be treated just like any other map. If it is a high resolution image, see the tips on reducing the size of the image in the Photos section in Chapter 17.

- Add labels on top of the map image to indicate the important places or areas. If you are indicating a single town or city, you can use a circle to show where it is and a text label to indicate the name. If you want the audience to focus on an area, such as a plot of land, use the drawing tools to draw a shape over that area, setting the fill to a semi-transparent color so that the underlying map is still somewhat visible. Add a text label to indicate the name or other identifying text for the area. If the text label will be hard to see on the map, add a semi-transparent fill color to the text box so the text is easier to read.

- Eliminate any distracting backgrounds of the map, or crop out areas that are not relevant for the point you are making. The less extraneous graphics there are on your slide, the easier it is for the audience to understand your point.

Screen Captures

Screen captures are used when you want to show the audience exactly what they will see on a program or website.

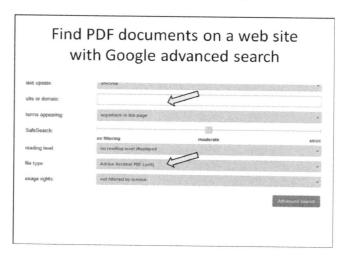

Best practices for using screen captures:

- To capture the entire screen, including any program icons, backgrounds, or toolbars, press the Print Screen key (sometimes abbreviated as Prnt Scrn or a similar shortened phrase). This will copy the current screen image to the Windows clipboard. Go to your PowerPoint slide, and paste the image on the slide. On a Mac, use the Command-Control-Shift-3 key combination.

- To capture only the single program you want to use, excluding other programs, icons, or toolbars, hold the Alt key down and press the Print Screen key. This will copy an image of only the current program screen to the Windows clipboard. You can now paste this image on your slide in PowerPoint. On a Mac, the equivalent key combination is Command-Control-Shift-4, and you can then select the application window you want copied to the clipboard.

- In some browsers, you can press the F11 key to get a clean view of a website, without toolbars, scrollbars or other program controls. This gives you a larger image and one that is easier to work with in PowerPoint.

- You can have even more control of what gets captured on the screen by using special screen capture software, such as SnagIt from TechSmith. This software, and others like it, allows you to select the exact screen region you want to capture and to alter the image prior to pasting it on your PowerPoint slide. This software is not needed for all purposes, but can be handy if your screen captures are more complex than the standard full screen or program only options built into the operating system.

- Once you have the screen capture image on your PowerPoint slide, you should use the cropping tool to crop out those portions of the image that you do not need. You should usually eliminate the scrollbars and any toolbars since they are not typically the focus of the screen capture. After the image has been cropped so that it contains only what you want, use the corner sizing handles to enlarge the image, making it easier for the audience to see.

- Most screen capture images will benefit from adding a callout to focus the audience's attention on one or two spots on the image. Use an arrow, circle, square, or other shape that draws attention to the most important part of the image. You can animate this callout shape so that it appears as you are speaking and makes your point more effectively. Callouts are discussed in more detail in Chapter 19.

- If you are using a screen capture of a website, consider adding a text label that contains the Web address (URL) so the audience can access that site later to take the action you are requesting. With so many of your audience members carrying mobile devices connected to the Internet, you may even have some access the website during your presentation.

PDF Content

PDF content is used when you have a table, diagram, image, text, or other content from an Adobe Acrobat PDF file that you want to include in your presentation as a graphic.

Example of Quick Method HST calculation for Alberta business

Quick Method calculation for Qwik Dry Cleaners Calgary, Alberta	
Calculation of GST remittance in first quarter of 2010 (3.6% remittance rate)	
Total eligible sales for the first quarter, including the GST (Qwik Dry would enter this amount on line 101 of its GST/HST return)	$ 22,000
Multiply the total eligible sales ($22,000) by the 3.6% remittance rate (Qwik Dry would enter this amount on line 103 of its GST/HST return)	$ 792
Deduct 1% for the first $30,000 of eligible sales (Qwik Dry would enter this amount on line 107 of its GST/HST return)	$ (220)
First quarter remittance (Qwik Dry would enter this amount on line 115 of its GST/HST return)	$ 572

Example from RC4058(E) Rev. 10

Best practices for including PDF content:

- You only need the freely available Adobe Acrobat Reader software to include PDF content on your slide. If you do not have this software, you can download it from Adobe's website at **www.adobe.com**.

- You want the best-looking graphic on your slide, so you want to capture the item from the PDF file at the highest resolution possible. To do so, make the Acrobat window as large as it can be on your screen and zoom in on the portion of the PDF document you want to use so it fills as much of the screen as possible. Since almost all PDF documents contain high-resolution text and graphics, you should not have a distorted image when zooming above 100% in Adobe Acrobat.

- Use the Snapshot tool to capture the portion of the PDF document you want to use. This tool is located on different menus depending on what version of Acrobat you have. It may be on the Tools menu, Select & Zoom sub-menu or it may be on the Edit menu. Once you select this tool, your cursor will change to a crosshairs drawing cursor (looks like a plus sign +). Click at one corner of the area you want to capture and drag the cursor to the opposite corner of the area, creating a rectangle around the portion you want to use. When you release the left mouse button, you will receive a message that the area has been copied to the Windows clipboard (you can select not to have this message come up if you prefer). Now go to your PowerPoint slide, and paste the image from the Windows clipboard.

- The copied item is treated in PowerPoint like a picture. Therefore you have all of the same tools you have when working with a picture, such as cropping, resizing, and even re-coloring. Position the graphic on the slide, and make it as large as it needs to be in order for the audience to easily see it.

- This technique can be useful for including a logo you have permission to use. Find a PDF document on the organization's website that includes a high-resolution logo you can capture using the snapshot tool.

- The only time that this technique will not work is if the PDF document has had copying disabled, which occurs in some purchased e-books or other documents.

Hyperlinks

A hyperlink is used when you want to go to the source of the information, whether it is a website or a file in another program.

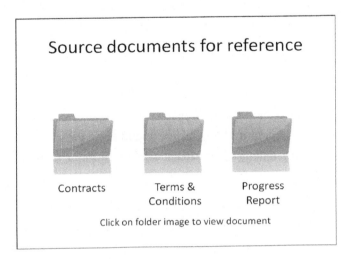

Best practices for using hyperlinks:

- Hyperlinks can be created on text, a shape, or an image. We usually see text hyperlinks on websites. Linking from a shape or image can leave your slide looking cleaner because there is less text, especially for website links that are very long.

- When you are linking to a website, you can use a screen capture of the site as the hyperlink so people get a preview of what will be shown. Consider putting the Web address on the slide as well, so that people can visit the site themselves after the presentation.

- If you are linking to a file, whether it is a document, spreadsheet, PDF file, or other file, the link must be made to a file that already exists. A hyperlink in PowerPoint cannot create a new document. Instead, create a document with just a title or single line of text in it, and link to that saved document.

- Hyperlinks can also be added to the Slide Master to allow access to a file at any time during the presentation. This technique is useful if you want to capture notes during the presentation for follow-up later on. The notes can be captured in a Word document and made available electronically right after the presentation is finished.

- Make sure that the file you are linking to will be accessible when you present. If the file is on a shared drive, copy it to a local location before you create the hyperlink. If you will be presenting from a different computer, put the linked file in the same folder as the PowerPoint file before you create the link. Make sure to copy the linked file along with the PowerPoint file when moving it to the other computer.

- In PowerPoint, there are two ways to activate a hyperlink during a slide show.

  - The first is to move the mouse over the hyperlink and click on the linked text/shape/image. This method can be distracting for the audience since they see the cursor moving across the slide, and it can cause stress for the presenter if they have to use a trackpad or other pointing device that they are not familiar with.

- The second is to use the Tab key to select the hyperlink (press the Tab key to highlight the hyperlink on the slide with a thin dashed outline), then press the Enter key to activate the link. This method still requires the presenter to access the keyboard, but it is less intrusive for the audience and easier for the presenter. If the slide has more than one hyperlink, each press of the Tab key will move the dashed outline highlight to the next hyperlink on the slide.

- When the hyperlink is activated, the linked file will open in the appropriate application as defined by the default settings in Windows. For example, Windows knows that an .XLS or .XLSX file is an Excel file, so it will automatically open Excel and then open the file. You can edit the file if you want to. For example, you can change a calculation in a spreadsheet in response to an audience question. The application is running on top of the slide show, so once you save the file and exit the application, you will automatically resume the slide show.

- Many programs, such as Word or Excel, are not natively meant to be projected in front of an audience. The default font sizes are usually far too small for the audience to easily read. Enlarge the font size in the saved file to at least 18 point before you start your presentation. If the font is still too small, practice increasing the font size or the zoom level in the program you will be using so that you can do it seamlessly during the presentation.

- After you have finished showing the file to the audience, save any changes you have made and exit the program. One quick way to exit almost any Windows program is to hold the Alt key and press the F4 key. This Alt+F4 key combination makes exiting a program quick and clean. Once the program has closed, you will be returned to your slide show and can continue from the slide you were last on.

Case studies/Success stories

In any presentation where you are selling ideas, products or services, your audience will want to know that you can actually solve their problem. Just stating that you can solve the problem is not enough, you have to provide proof. One of the best ways to prove your capabilities is by sharing examples of past situations where you successfully solved similar problems. I call these case studies or success stories. I have a four-part formula for creating these powerful stories.

Before I get to the four steps, I want to emphasize the reason you should consider using case studies. It is not to brag about the work you have done. Too often I see presenters use case studies as a way to boast about the big name clients they have worked for. Remember the focus is not on impressing the audience, it is on trying to find the best solution to their problem. This means that all of your case studies need to be selected because they illustrate your ability to solve a problem that is similar to the one faced by this audience. The similarity should be in one of three areas: it is a similar industry/organization, it is a similar challenge that is being faced, or it is a similar solution being recommended.

The first step in creating a case study or success story is to describe the problem. Make sure you show how it is similar to the problem this audience is struggling with. In a consulting assignment, I suggested that my client choose a case where they had dealt with a significant slope on a piece of property, since that was a major concern for their client. If the case study does not directly relate to the situation they face, the audience is confused as to why you are sharing it.

The second step is to measure the size of the problem that was being faced. Every organization has more problems than they have resources to solve. The ones that get attention are the ones that are deemed big enough or important enough. Provide a measurement of what this problem was costing, what difficulties were being encountered, or the significance of the challenge. This shows the audience that you have experience dealing with the size of problem they are currently facing.

The third step is to give an overview of the solution you provided in the case. Do not think that you need to go into a lot of detail with this explanation. Keep it at a high level so they do not get overwhelmed by detail. The details of the solution for this audience will, of course, be different, so keep the discussion to the major activities or approaches you used. If you feel it necessary, have hidden backup slides with additional detail in case the audience asks for more details on the solution.

In the final step, provide a measurement of the impact of the solution. Show how it benefitted the organization that was having the problem. As much as possible, show the impact using the same measures as in step two, when you described the size of the problem. You can talk about cost reduction, revenue increase, increase in measures of customer satisfaction, or any other relevant measures for the situation at hand. The audience wants to see that your solution actually made a difference, so make that clear.

By following these four steps, you can show the audience that you have the experience to solve the type of problem they have, the size of problem they have, and provide a solution that has a positive impact on results.

You can recap the case study on one slide or on multiple slides in your presentation, depending on the level of detail you feel necessary to share for this audience and their problem. Use various visuals such as photos, diagrams, comparison tables, or video testimonials to reinforce the details of the case.

CHAPTER NINETEEN

Adding Callouts

A visual is more intuitively understood than a slide full of text, but if the audience is not able to determine the most important part of the visual, they may take away a different message from the one you intended. A callout directs the audience's attention to the most important part of the visual. Callouts eliminate the presenter using a pointing device or laser pointer to try to highlight important areas on a visual. When a presenter uses a pointing device or walks to the screen and points at parts of the screen, it is distracting and ineffective for a number of reasons.

Why are laser pointers a problem for many audience members? Here are five reasons:

1. Many people can't see the small dot of a laser pointer on the screen due to its size and the lighting in the room.

2. It is virtually impossible to hold a laser pointer exactly still, and the movement on the screen naturally distracts people to look at the movement instead of listening to you.

3. The only way to hold the laser dot in the correct place is to face the screen, but then you end up speaking to the screen instead of the audience.

4. People who later get the presentation by e-mail won't know that you were pointing at all.

5. People viewing the presentation over the Web/video link can't see what you are pointing at, since they aren't in the room to see the laser dot.

If you walk to the screen and point with a stick or your arm, you almost always end up walking in front of the projected image, blocking some of the visual and reducing the context for the audience. Depending on how the screen is set up and where the image is on the screen, you may be unable to physically reach the intended spot on the screen and you end up pointing to a different spot while trying to get the audience to look elsewhere on the slide.

Both, using a laser pointer and walking to point at the screen, result in more audience confusion and less clarity of your message.

Instead of using a laser pointer, design your slides with callouts which you build one by one. Callouts allow you to face the audience the entire time, don't distract with movement, are big enough to see, and are part of the slide so anyone viewing the slide over the Web or following the live presentation will know what your callout was pointing to. The callout shows the audience where the most important part of the visual is and why this part is so important.

The first part of the callout is the graphic highlight. This is usually an arrow, circle, box, or some other graphic that is added to indicate where the audience should focus their attention. Many presenters know that a graphic highlight is helpful when using visuals.

The second part of the callout is the callout text, and this is what too many presenters forget. The callout text explains in words to the audience why you added the graphic highlight. Without the callout text, the audience won't know why they are supposed to look at the area being highlighted. And they may actually come to the wrong conclusion.

Here is an example of a slide with a callout.

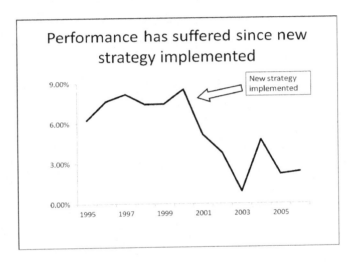

Best practices for creating graphic highlights:

- The greatest challenge when creating a graphic highlight is selecting a color for the highlight that will have enough contrast with the underlying colors of the slide or the parts of the visual. This can often be difficult because the colors of a visual will contrast with the slide background; finding another color that contrasts with both is very hard. If you can find a single color to use for a graphic highlight, ensure that the highlight is thick enough to be easily seen. A minimum thickness of three points is usually a good guideline to use.

- If there are multiple colors that will be behind the graphic highlight, use a combination of colors in the graphic highlight to ensure contrast in all areas. A technique that works well is to use or create a graphic highlight that has a thick black outline and a bright yellow interior. This ensures that in dark background areas the bright yellow is easily seen and in light background areas the black is visible.

- If your slide software does not allow you to create a shape that has two colors in the outline, you can create your own shape. You can create a shape, such as a rounded rectangle, that has contrast in itself, from two rounded rectangles. To do this, draw the first rectangle with no fill color and a thick (12 point) black outline. Make a copy of this rectangle. The second rectangle is set to have a bright yellow thinner (six point) outline. The second rectangle is then moved on top of the first rectangle, making it appear that a single rectangle has two contrasting colors as the outline. This technique of contrasting colors will allow a graphic callout to be seen in every situation.

- Try to position the graphic highlight so that it does not cover up too much of the underlying visual. If too much of the visual is obscured, the audience will lose context. For lines or arrows, extend them so that the tail is far enough away that the text you add will not cover up much of the visual. For shapes, such as ovals or rectangles, you may need to add a line that extends away from the visual to connect the relevant text to the shape. If the shape must cover up a part of the visual, consider using a semi-transparent fill color for the shape so that the underlying visual can be partially seen.

- PowerPoint has built-in callout shapes which contain an area to add the callout text. These shapes can work well when you don't have a lot of room on the slide to add the callout.

Best practices for creating callout text:

- Use a separate text box for the callout text instead of using an existing text box or placeholder. This allows you to format and position the text exactly where you want it to be. Size the text box to contain the text and little else, so that it is compact and not overly large.

- Choose a font that is at least 18 point or larger, so that the text is easily read when projected or printed in handout form.

- If the text must be placed on top of the visual, you may have the challenge of finding a text color that will contrast with the variety of colors in the visual underneath the text. The best solution is to fill the text box with a contrasting color, so that the text is easily seen, but make the fill semi-transparent so that the audience can still faintly see the underlying visual. This allows the text to be read while still maintaining the context of the visual underneath.

CHAPTER TWENTY

Building Information To Keep Audience Focus

If you display a slide all at once, the audience may not know where to look first and they will spend time trying to figure out the slide before they start listening to you. Displaying everything on the slide at the start also does not give you an opportunity to set the right context or explain some concepts in a certain sequence. By building the elements of the slide, you have the opportunity to speak to each part of the slide and give it the proper attention it deserves.

For example, when you are speaking about a column graph, you will likely want to build each column one at a time so that you can speak about the meaning of that column. In a process diagram, you would build each step in the process to be able to explain that step and how it fits in to the overall point you are making. If you have four points you want to make in a text list, you would build the points one by one so you can fully discuss one point before moving on to the next point.

One way to create the building of elements on a slide is to create multiple slides, each with one more element added to the overall visual. While this works, it is usually more time-consuming to create and harder to work with when you want to make changes, because you have to change multiple slides. Use this method only if a web presentation system does not support PowerPoint's Animation feature.

PowerPoint Animation

An easier way to build elements on a slide is to use the Animation feature of PowerPoint. This feature allows you to select any element on the slide and give instructions on when and how that element should appear on the slide.

While I am suggesting you use the Animation feature to build the points on your slides, why is it that so much of the animation we see annoys us? This occurs because the presenter went for entertainment value instead of remembering that they should be making the point clear to the audience. PowerPoint includes fancy animation effects that enable you to make an element fly, twirl or bounce on the slide. Too often, presenters get seduced by these "cool" effects and include them in their presentations. The unfortunate result is that these "cool" effects actually annoy and distract the audience. They will tune out quickly if they perceive an "amateur" quality to the presentation. Save the fancy effects for humorous or entertaining slides at your next family event.

When using the animation feature of PowerPoint to build the elements of your slide, here are some best practices to keep in mind:

- To avoid annoying the audience, use simple animation effects only. Suggestions include:

  - Making text, shapes, or images simply appear using the Appear, Fade or Dissolve effects.

  - Using the Peek In or Wipe effect to show an arrow or line moving towards the spot you want the audience to focus on.

- Sequence the elements in the correct order, so that you can logically build the visual with your explanation. PowerPoint allows you to bring more than one element on the slide at the same time using the "With Previous" or "After Previous" timing controls. Before you start animating elements on the slide, take some time to think through the sequence that will make the most sense to the audience.

- When building a series of bullet points or the parts of a graph, use the animation Options in PowerPoint to get the sequence you want. For bullet point lists, you can set what levels of bullets come on at once. On a graph, you can set whether each data point comes on individually or whether a series comes on together.

- Always test the animations and the sequence before you deliver your presentation to make sure that your message is logically supported by the visual. Test how the effect looks, the sequence of animation, and the speed and direction of any movement effects.

- Do not use the automatic timing or pre-set animation features of PowerPoint. Having movement or building pre-set by the software reduces the control you have over your presentation and can cause difficulties when presenting.

Exit Animation Reveal Technique

If you need to build parts of a visual that the usual entrance animation effects won't work on, you may be able to achieve the same result using exit animation of overlying shapes.

This approach reveals the key information you want the audience to see by sequentially removing shapes that are covering each part of the visual. It is like we used to do with overhead transparencies. We covered up the transparency with a piece of paper and revealed each part by sliding the paper off one area at a time.

The best way to implement this technique is to use the transparent background method I first saw demonstrated by PowerPoint MVP Glen Millar. This method uses the ability to fill a shape with the background of the slide. First, draw a shape on the slide, for example a rectangle, covering up the element or portion of the element you want to reveal. Format the shape so that it has no outline and the fill effect is set to "Background." If you are covering up a graph or other element that has a background different from the slide (such as a white background on a graph or imported image), set the shape color to the background of the underlying element. In the animation task pane, apply an exit animation to this image so that when you advance, the image is removed from the slide, revealing what is underneath. Using this approach, you can achieve the building of the elements on the slide in the order that you want to discuss them in.

The only downside to this method is that when you print the slide, the shape covers up the underlying element and it appears that there is nothing there on the slide. To get around this, create a duplicate hidden slide that does not use this technique. Print this hidden slide instead of the slide you use for presenting.

Additional Advanced Animation Techniques

One challenge with using animation to build an image is that the single image does not contain multiple pieces you can bring on one at a time. In this situation, you may be able to break the image into multiple parts in order to create the effect you want. Generally, you can only break an image into pieces that are rectangular. To do so, make copies of the image and use the Align feature to layer them on top of one another. Select the top image and use the Crop tool to reduce it to the piece that you want to appear last in the build sequence. Select the image in the next layer down and use the Crop tool to reduce it to the piece you want to appear second last. Continue selecting layers and cropping them until you have created multiple pieces of the image. Now you can use the simple animation techniques described earlier to build the entire image from the pieces you have created.

In some situations you need to show a more complex image or diagram in order to set the context, but then you want to focus the audience's attention on only one part of the visual. In this case, it may be best to cover up the portions of the visual that you want to de-emphasize. You can do this with a semi-transparent shape. I suggest making the shape semi-transparent because if the shape is a solid color, the audience may lose the context when they can no longer see the rest of the visual.

Use a Presentation Remote

Once you start building your slides point by point and building the visuals piece by piece, you will quickly find that you are tied to your computer to advance each build unless you use a presentation remote.

A presentation remote allows you to advance your builds and slides without having to be physically close to your laptop. There are many models of remotes available, ranging from simple ones that just provide movement of slides up to ones that allow full mouse control and even have timers to track how long you have left in the time allotted for your presentation. They work by having a receiver attached to a USB port on your computer and the remote in your hand communicating with the receiver to transfer your commands to the program.

I suggest that unless you really need full mouse control or the other features, you stick with a simple version of a remote. The remote that I use only has four buttons: forward, backward, blank the screen, and a laser pointer. I don't need more than these functions.

When I started bringing my remote with me, one helpful tip I learned from professional speaker Ed Rigsbee was to remove one or both batteries from the remote before you pack it in your computer case. This way, a button won't get accidentally pushed when in the case and drain your batteries (yes, this has happened to me).

Once you use a presentation remote and see how much more effective you are as a presenter by using it to build the elements on your slide, you'll wonder why you went so long without one.

CHAPTER TWENTY-ONE

Drilling Down Into Complex Information

Sometimes you will have to present complex information, and it is especially important that any complex visuals are made easy for the audience to understand. I wrote in Chapter 18 about how hyperlinks can be used to jump to detailed information contained in other files or hidden slides. There are two additional techniques that will help you keep the audience on track and understanding your message, even if part of it is complex.

The Break Down and Zoom In Technique

This technique works well when you want to show a complex visual, for example a financial statement, and then look at specific areas one at a time to understand what each area means to the audience. Here is how you can use this technique:

- Start by showing the entire visual. This is crucial so that the audience has context for what you want to say. It is also helpful if they have the visual in their handout or other printed information because they can easily identify what you are about to discuss.

- Next, indicate on the visual the different areas that you will be examining in more detail. You can do this with callout shapes. I find that using semi-transparent rectangles works well, with text in the shape that indicates the name of the area or section.

- Now you can move to slides that show the detail of each area one at a time. Because this is a much smaller segment of the entire visual, it is no longer complex and can be more easily explained. Have a separate slide to show each detailed area that you outlined in the previous step.

- At any time during your explanation, you can always return to the overall visual if you feel you need to remind the audience of where you are and reset their context. This doesn't need to happen after every detailed area explanation, only when you feel it would help the audience.

The Zoom In on a Portion Technique

This technique works well when you want to examine just one area of a complex visual. For example, if you have a screen capture of a website and you want to zoom in on one link so the audience knows where to find a link for more information. Here are the steps to using this technique:

- Show the entire visual at the start. This sets the context and allows them to identify what they are first looking at.

- Use a callout shape, usually a rectangle or oval shape, to show where you want the audience to focus their attention.

- Then, on top of the original visual, bring on a larger view of just that one section of the visual. The easiest way to create this larger image is to copy the original image and use the cropping tools to eliminate the parts you don't need to focus on. Resize this section so it is larger and easier to see. I also recommend that you use a black outline around the section so it is easy to distinguish from the entire visual underneath. Using the Faded Zoom animation effect to bring this section on the screen gives the audience the feeling that they are actually zooming in on this section for a closer look.

- I find it useful to leave the original visual behind the zoomed in section to give the audience context.

- You can now discuss this section in the detail it requires, and you can use callouts on this section if it aids in your explanation.

SECTION FOUR

How To Start Using These Ideas

I know that I have shared a lot of information in this book. It may seem overwhelming to think of trying to use all of what I have shared in your next presentation. Please don't even try to do that, it won't work. I share a lot of content in my workshops and the participants find it helpful to have some guidelines on how to best start implementing this information. Here are some steps that will help you create more effective presentations and ensure the audience "gets it":

1. Focus on planning your message using the RAPIDS approach. Even if you were to use no slides at all, your audience will appreciate a well structured and thought through message. When you are applying the RAPIDS approach, start small with just mapping the outline of the presentation after you decide on the goal and analyze the audience. As you develop more presentations, develop the more detailed outline with each slide planned individually.

2. If information overload is your biggest issue, focus on applying the strategies in that section of the RAPIDS approach. Work on a few slides and see how much clearer they can be for your audience.

3. Write headlines for your slides. This is the easiest thing you can do to improve the focus of your slides, the focus of your message, and help identify what can be eliminated from an overloaded presentation.

4. Start by looking at the one or two slides that you feel are not connecting well with the audience. Apply what you have learned in this book to determine what may help those slides improve. Make the changes and see how it goes. By improving the worst part of your presentation, the whole presentation gets better.

5. Only tackle a few slides at a time when you are moving from mainly text slides to using visuals. It is too much work to redo all of your slides at once and you will give up. Instead, work on just one section of your presentation and create effective visuals for those few slides. Next time you present, select another section to work on. It may take six to twelve months to address all of your slides, but you will do it at a pace that is reasonable.

6. Get technical training if you need to become more comfortable with whatever software you are using. If your skills at PowerPoint or other presentation software are holding you back, get the training you need to improve your skills. I list some training resources later in this chapter. Take advantage of the vast quantity of education available on the web.

7. Rehearse more. The best way to be confident when presenting is to rehearse what you are going to say so that you are comfortable with it. Book the time in your schedule for rehearsals and don't let anything prevent you from this important task.

8. Celebrate your successes. As you see small improvements, note them and take a moment to celebrate. This will motivate you to continue using what

you have learned in this book to create more effective presentations in the future.

How to evaluate your presentations

Part of continually improving your presentations is to evaluate past presentations. The best way is to watch a video of your presentation. You can self-evaluate using these tips:

- *Get different perspectives*: set up the video camera in different places so you can see how you come across from a variety of viewpoints. You may discover that someone at the back of the room sees your presentation very differently from someone at the front of the room.

- *Message structure*: Was the goal clear? How accurate was your audience analysis? Did the audience look lost at any time during your presentation? Did you get the glazed eyes look from information overload? Were some questions related to not understanding what should have already been clear?

- *Flow of delivery*: Was there a smooth flow between your points? Did you move comfortably during the presentation? Did you get heads nodding along the way indicating they were understanding the points?

- *Use of emotions & stories*: Did you appear relaxed because you felt totally prepared? Did you use examples and stories to make the points connect with the audience? Did you show emotion through your body language?

If you want to take your presentations up to the next level, consider getting professional coaching in presentation creation and delivery. Find a coach who you are comfortable with and who comes well recommended by the people they have helped. I regularly invest in coaching to keep my skills evolving and improving.

Online resources for further information

Part of my efforts to improve the effectiveness of presentations is developing and making information available for presenters at all stages of their experience. My website, **www.ThinkOutsideTheSlide.com**, contains hundreds of free resources, including:

- *Articles:* I cover a wide range of presentation topics in the articles I have written, from preparation to delivery.

- *Newsletter:* I have been writing my bi-weekly newsletter for over ten years and all of the back issues are archived on my site. You can sign up for your own free subscription on the website.

- ***PowerPoint Video Tutorials:*** I have over 30 video tutorials you can use to learn many of the techniques I mention in this book. Download them to your computer and watch along, pausing at any time to try the technique on your version of PowerPoint.

- ***Slide Makeover Videos:*** There are over 70 examples of slide makeovers, where you see the "before" slide, the "after" slide" and hear me explain the lessons you can learn from the makeover. Customized makeovers are always the highlight of my workshops, with my clients using the makeovers I show and these makeover videos to reinforce their learning.

- *Tutorials by PowerPoint MVPs:* These include getting started with PowerPoint and PowerPoint for the Mac.

- *Color Contrast Calculator:* A tool referred to in Chapter 10 that allows you to determine if two colors have enough contrast using the two international standard tests.

- *Font Size Charts:* I have calculated what font size is easy to see based on the size of the screen and the size of the room. These charts are described in Chapter 10.

- *Recommended Resources:* Resources include the PowerPoint FAQ site for detailed answers to more technical questions

Final words

My encouragement would be to just start. Start in whatever way makes sense for you. You **can** be more successful with your presentations. It is possible. It will take some effort, there is no doubt about that. But anything worth improving takes time and effort. I look forward to hearing the success you experience in your future presentations.

Index

Training & Consulting Services

I develop and deliver customized training sessions for teams who want to improve their skills in creating and delivering effective PowerPoint presentations that their audience will understand. The ideas get implemented because I always show makeovers of actual slides the team is using. I also work with professionals and executives on high-stakes presentations to create a clear message and persuasive visuals to accompany the presenter.

How is the training and consulting that I do different from other services you may consider? Typical presentation training and consulting falls into one of three areas: technical PowerPoint courses, stand up presentation skills, or designing a prettier set of slides. If those are the skills you need, that is great. I can suggest experts in these areas. But if your PowerPoint presentations are not getting your message across effectively, technical how-to information, speaking skills, or fancy graphics won't help you. That's why my training and consulting helps you craft a clear message using effective slides that is easy to deliver and gets results.

On my website you can see case studies, read testimonials, and see my extensive client list. When you are ready to take the next step in making your PowerPoint presentations more effective, contact me.

Phone: (905) 510-4911 (Eastern North America time zone)

E-mail: Dave@ThinkOutsideTheSlide.com

Web: www.ThinkOutsideTheSlide.com